THREE INTRODUCTORY LECTURES
ON THE
SCIENCE OF THOUGHT

THREE INTRODUCTORY LECTURES

ON THE

SCIENCE OF THOUGHT

BY

F. MAX MULLER

WITH A CORRESPONDENCE ON "THOUGHT WITHOUT WORDS" BETWEEN F. MAX MULLER AND FRANCIS GALTON, THE DUKE OF ARGYLL, GEORGE J. ROMANES, AND OTHERS.

GYAN

Published by

GYAN

Gyan Publishing House
5, Ansari Road
Daryaganj, New Delhi-110002
Phone: 011-47034999, 9811692060
E-mail: books@gyanbooks.com

Distribution Network
gyanbooks.com
India, USA, Canada, UK, Australia, France

ISBN : 978-81-212-3849-6 (PB)
First Published, 1898

2nd Impression 2020

Printed at: Gyan Press, Delhi.

Science of Thought
Author: F. Max Muller

THREE INTRODUCTORY LECTURES

ON THE

SCIENCE OF THOUGHT

BY

F. MAX MÜLLER

WITH A CORRESPONDENCE ON "THOUGHT WITHOUT WORDS" BETWEEN F. MAX MÜLLER AND FRANCIS GALTON, THE DUKE OF ARGYLL, GEORGE J. ROMANES, AND OTHERS.

CHICAGO
THE OPEN COURT PUBLISHING COMPANY
FOR SALE BY
KEGAN PAUL, TRENCH, TRÜBNER & CO., Ltd., LONDON
1898

PREFACE.

Though the three lectures on the "Science of Thought," which I delivered in March, 1887, at the Royal Institution in London, and which were afterwards published in *The Open Court*, hardly require a preface, being themselves a kind of preface or introduction to a larger work on the same subject,* yet as I had just been writing to a friend of mine in answer to several questions which he had addressed to me on the principal purpose of my book, I gladly give here a few extracts from that letter, which may serve to prepare the reader for what he has to expect in this small volume.

You tell me that my book on the Science of Thought is thoroughly revolutionary, and that I have all recognized authorities in philosophy against me. I doubt it. My book is, if you like, evolutionary, but not revolutionary. I mean it is the natural outcome of that philosophical and historical study of language, which began with Leibniz, and which during our century has so widely spread and ramified as to overshadow nearly all sciences, not excepting what I call the Science of Thought. If you mean by revolutionary a violent breaking with the past, I hold on the contrary that a full appreciation of the true nature of language and a recognition of its inseparableness from thought will prove the best means of recovering that unbroken thread, which binds our modern schools of thought most closely together with those of the Middle Ages and of ancient Greece. It alone will help us to

* *The Science of Thought*, by F. Max Müller. London: Longmans, Green & Co., 1887.

reconcile systems of philosophy hitherto supposed to be entirely antagonistic. If I am right—and I must confess that with regard to the fundamental principle of the identity of reason and language I share the common weakness of all philosophers that I cannot doubt its truth—then what we call the history of philosophy will assume a totally new aspect. It will reveal itself before our eyes as the natural growth of language, though at the same time as a constant struggle of old against new language, in fact, as a dialectic process, in the true sense of the word.

The very tenet that language is identical with thought, what is it but a correction of language, a repentance, a return of language upon itself? We have two words, and therefore it requires with us a strong effort to perceive that behind these two words there is but one essence. To a Greek this effort would be comparatively easy, because the word *Logos* continued to mean the undivided essence of language and thought. In our modern languages we shall find it difficult to coin a word that could take the place of *Logos*. Neither *discours* in French, nor *Rede* in German, which meant originally the same as *ratio*, will help us. We shall have to be satisfied with such compounds as thought-word or word-thought. At least I can think of no better expedient.

You strongly object to my saying that there is no such thing as reason. But let us see whether we came honestly by that word. Because we reason, that is, because we reckon, because we add and subtract, therefore we say that we have reason, and thus it happened that reason was raised into something which we have or possess, into a faculty, or power, or something, whatever it may be, that deserves to be written with a capital R. And yet we have only to look into the workshop of language in order to see that there is nothing substantial corresponding to this substantive, and that neither the heart nor the brain, neither the breath nor the spirit of man discloses its original whereabouts. It may sound violent and revolutionary to you when I say that there is no such thing as reason, and yet no philosopher, not even Kant, has ever in his definition of reason told us what it is really made of. But remember, I am far from saying that Reason is a mere word. That expression, "a mere word," seems to me the most objectionable expression in the whole of our philosophical dictionary.

Reason is something, namely language, not simply as we now hear it and use it, but as it has been slowly elaborated by man through all the ages of his existence on earth. Reason is the growth of centuries, it is the work of man, and at the same time an instrument brought to higher and higher perfection by the leading thinkers and speakers of the world. No reason without language, no language without reason. Try to reckon without numbers, whether spoken, written, or otherwise marked, and if you succeed in that, I shall admit that it is possible to reason or reckon without words, and that there is in us such a thing, or such a power or faculty, as reason, apart from words.

You say I shall never live to see it admitted that man cannot reason without words. This does not discourage me. Through the whole of my life I have cared for truth, not for success. And truth is not our own. We may seek truth, serve truth, love truth; but truth takes care of herself, and she inspires her true lovers with the same feeling of perfect trust. Those who cannot believe in themselves, unless they are believed in by others, have never known what truth is. Those who have found truth, know best how little it is their work, and how small the merit which they can claim for themselves. They were blind before, and now they can see. That is all.

But even if I thought that truth depended on majorities, I believe I might boldly say that the majority of philosophers of all ages and countries is really on my side,* though few only have asserted the identity of reason and language without some timorous reserve, still fewer have seen all the consequences that flow from it.

Some people seem to resent it almost as a personal insult that what we call our divine reason should be no more than human language, and that the whole of this human language should have been derived from no more than 800 roots, which can be reduced to about 120 concepts. But if I had wished to startle my readers, I could easily have shown that out of these 800 roots, one-half could really have been dispensed with, and has been dispensed with in modern languages,† while among the 120 concepts not a few are clearly secondary, and owe their place in my list ‡ merely to the fact that in Sanskrit they cannot be reduced to any more primitive concepts. To dance, for instance, cannot be called a primitive concept; perhaps not even to hunger, to thirst, to cook,

---

* See *Science of Thought*, p. 31 seq.

† Ibid., p. 417.

‡ Ibid., p. 619.

to roast, etc. Only it so happens that in Sanskrit, to which my statistical remarks were restricted, we cannot go behind such roots as NÆRT, KSHUDH, TÆRSH, PAK, etc. It is in that limited sense only that such roots and such concepts can be called primitive. The number of really primitive concepts would be so alarmingly small that for the present it seemed wiser to say nothing about it. But so far from being ashamed of our modest beginnings, we ought really to glory rather in having raised our small patrimony to the immense wealth now hoarded in our dictionaries.

When we once know what our small original patrimony consisted in, the question how we came in possession of it, may seem of less importance. Yet it is well to remember that the theory of the origin of roots and concepts, as propounded by Noiré, differs, not by degrees, but *toto cœlo* from the old attempts to derive roots from interjections and imitations of natural sounds. That a certain number of words in every language has been derived from interjections and imitations, no one has ever denied. But such words are not conceptual words, and they become possible only after language had become possible, that is, after man had reached his power of forming concepts. No man who has not himself grappled with that problem, can appreciate the complete change that has come over it by the recognition of the fact that roots are the phonetic expressions of the consciousness of our own acts. Nothing but this our consciousness of our own repeated acts could possibly have given us our first concepts. Nothing else answers the necessary requirement of a concept that it should be the consciousness of something manifold, yet necessarily realized as one. After the genesis of the first concept, everything else becomes intelligible. The results of our acts become the first objects of our conceptual thought, and with conceptual thought language, which is nothing if not conceptual, begins. Roots are afterwards localized and made the signs of our objects by means of local exponents, whether suffixes, prefixes, or infixes. What has been scraped and shaped again and again becomes as it were "shape-here," i. e. a shaft; what has been dug and hollowed out by repeated blows, becomes "dig-here," i. e. a hole. And from the concept of a hole dug, or of an empty cave there is an uninterrupted progress to the most abstract concepts such as empty space or even nothing. No doubt, when we hear the sound of cuckoo, we may by one jump arrive at the word cuckoo. This may be called a word, but it is not a conceptual word, and we deal with conceptual words only.

Before we can get at a single conceptual word, we have to pass through at least five stages:

(1) Consciousness of our own repeated acts;

(2) *Clamor concomitans* of these acts;

(3) Consciousness of that *clamor* as concomitant of the act;

(4) Repetition of that *clamor* to recall the act;

(5) *Clamor* (root) defined by prefixes, suffixes, etc., to recall the act as localized in its results, its instruments, its agents, etc.

You can see from my preface to *The Science of Thought*, that I was quite prepared for fierce attacks, whether they came from theologians, from philosophers, or from a certain class of scholars. So far from being discouraged, I am really delighted by the opposition which my book has roused, though you would be surprised to hear what strong support also I have received from quarters where I least expected it. I have never felt called upon to write a book to which everybody should say *Amen*. When I write a book, I expect the world to say *tamen*, as I have said *tamen* to the world. I have been called very audacious for daring to interfere with philosophy, as if the study of language, to which I have devoted the whole of my life, could be separated from a study of philosophy. Professors of philosophy are happily not the only philosophers in the world. I have listened very patiently for many years to the old story that grammar is one thing and logic another; that the former deals with such laws of thought as are observed, the latter with such as ought to be observed. No, no. True philosophy teaches us another lesson, namely that nothing is except what ought to be, and that in the evolution of the mind as well as in that of nature, natural selection is in reality rational selection. We must learn to recognize in language the true evolution of reason. In that evolution nothing is real and remains real except what is rational, and even the apparently irrational and anomalous has its reason and justification. Towards the end of the last century what used to be called *Grammaire Générale* formed a very favorite subject for academic discussions; it has now been replaced by what may be called *Grammaire Historique*. In the same manner *Formal Logic*, or the study of the general laws of thought, will have to make room for *Historical Logic*, or a study of the historical growth of thought. Delbrück's essays on comparative syntax show what can be done in this direction. For practical purposes, for teaching the art of reasoning, Formal Logic will always retain its separate existence; but the best study of the real laws of thought will be hereafter the study of real laws of language. If it was indeed so very audacious to make the identity of language and reason the foundation of a new system of philosophy, may I make the modest request that some philosopher by profession should give us a definition of what language is without reason, or reason without language.

In writing thus unreservedly to a friend I have perhaps spoken of myself and my work with greater freedom than I should have done in addressing the public at large. But as the public, and more especially the American public, has been a friend to me for many years, I hope I may be forgiven for having addressed it as a friend, and having counted on its sympathy and forbearance.

F. MAX MÜLLER.

Oxford, September 2, 1887.

THE SIMPLICITY OF LANGUAGE.

It is more than a quarter of a century since I ventured for the first time (June, 1861) to address the members of the Royal Institution, and I well remember the feeling of fear and trembling that came over me when in this very place I began to deliver my first lecture on the Science of Language as one of the physical sciences. I was young then, and to find myself face to face with such an audience as this Institution always attracts, was indeed a severe trial. As I looked round to see who was present, I met in one place the keen dark eyes of Faraday, in another the massive face of the Bishop of St. David's, in another the kind and thoughtful features of Frederick Maurice, while I was cheered with a look of recognition and encouragement from dear Stanley. I could mention several more names, "men, take them all in all, we shall not look upon their like again." To address such an audience on a subject that could never be popular, and without any of those charming experiments which enliven the discourses of most lecturers in this room, was an ordeal indeed. But painful as the ordeal was, I do not regret having passed through it. Many of my most valued friendships date from that time, and though in advocating a new cause and running full tilt against many time-honored prejudices, one cannot always avoid making enemies also, yet I feel that I owe a large debt of gratitude to this Institution, and not to my kind friends only, but likewise to my honest opponents.

It is hardly remembered now that before the time when I boldly claimed a place among the physical sciences for what I called the Science of Language, Comparative Philology was treated only as a kind of appendix to classical scholarship, and that even that place was grudged to it by some of the most eminent students of Greek and Latin. No doubt, the works of Bopp, Grimm, Pott, Benfey, Curtius, Schleicher, had at that time attracted attention in England, and the labors of such scholars as Donaldson, Latham, Garret and others, could well claim a place by their side for originality, honesty of purpose and clearness of sight. But there is a difference between Comparative Philology and what I meant by the Science of Language. Comparative Philology is the means, the Science of Language is the end.

We must begin with a careful analytical and comparative study of languages; we must serve our apprenticeship as phoneticians, etymologists and grammarians, before we can venture to go beyond. In this respect I am as great a pedant as ever, and shall rather continue to be taunted as such than abate one iota from my implicit faith in phonetic laws. What I said years ago in my lectures on the Science of Language, that phonetics must form the foundation of Comparative Philology, and that the laws which determine the changes of vowels and consonants are as unchangeable as the laws which regulate the circulation of our blood, may have been a little exaggerated, but in this respect exaggeration is decidedly better than the smallest concession. I also hold still to another heresy of mine, for which I have been much abused, namely that a knowledge of Sanskrit is a *sine qua non* for every comparative philologist, whether his special subject be Aryan, Semitic, or Turanian philology. I know it has been the fashion of late to cry down the importance of Sanskrit, because it does not supply the key to all secrets, and because in some, nay, in many cases, Sanskrit is less primitive than Greek, or Irish, or Gothic. This is a capital lesson to learn, and may, I hope, put an end at last to the false position which Sanskrit still occupies in the eyes of certain scholars, as the fountain head of all Aryan speech. But with all this, Sanskrit will always maintain its pre-eminence, as affording the best discipline to the student of language; and we have only to compare the works of those who have mastered Sanskrit, and of those who have not, whether they treat of Greek, or Latin, or Armenian, or Albanian, in order to perceive the immense difference between the scholar who sails with a safe compass and the bold adventurer who trusts to the stars.

Comparative Philology is a delightful subject, and the more it is cultivated the more fascinating it becomes, by the very minuteness of the laws and rules which govern its proceedings. There is enough in it to absorb a man's whole mind, enough to occupy a whole life. But for all that, we must not forget that the study of languages has an object beyond itself, a wider purpose, a higher aim.

And what is that higher purpose which the Science of Language is meant to serve? It is to discover the secrets of thought in the labyrinth of language, after the dark chambers of that labyrinth have first been lighted up by the torch of Comparative Philology. If there are any here present who attended my former courses on the Science of Language, delivered in this Institution, they will remember how often I appealed to the philosophers, whether logicians, physiologists, or metaphysicians, inviting them to a study of language which, like the thread of Ariadne, would lead them safely through the intricate passages of the human mind, through which they had been groping their way for so many centuries, without ever meeting the monster which they meant to slay. In my lectures on Comparative Mythology, in particular, I tried to show the irresistible influence which language, in its growth and decay, has exercised on thought, not only in what is commonly called mythology, the stories of gods and heroes, but in every sphere of knowledge, call it religion, philosophy, science, or anything else. We may do what we like, our thoughts are always hide-bound in language, and it is this inevitable phase of thought and language, inevitable in every branch of knowledge, which I meant by mythology, using that word in a far wider sense than had ever before been assigned to it. In order to make my meaning quite clear, and to provoke, if possible, contradiction, that is independent thought, I called mythology a disease of language, though adding at the same time that it was to be considered as an infantine disease, as a natural crisis through which our intellectual constitution must pass in order to maintain its health and vigor. Now it is curious that those who expressed their agreement with me that mythology, including metaphysics, might indeed be considered as a disease of language, did not ask themselves what in that case the health of language would mean. Right language is right thought, and right thought is right language; and if we want to understand, not only the disease, but the health also of our thought, that is to say, the whole life of our thought, we can study it nowhere more efficiently than in the pathology of language.

The Science of Language, therefore, was to me at all time but a means to an end—a telescope to watch the heavenly movements of our thoughts, a microscope to discover the primary cells of our concepts. I have waited for many years, hoping that some one better qualified than myself might lay hold of the materials collected by the comparative philologists, and build with them a new system of philosophy. Everything was ready—the ore was there, it had only to be coined. But whether philosophers mistrusted the ore, or whether they preferred to speculate with their time-honored tokens rather than with the genuine metal, certain it is that, with few exceptions, no philosopher by profession has as yet utilized the new facts which the Science of Language has placed at his free disposal.

I know the answer that will be made. The results of the Science of Language, it has often been said, are as yet so unsettled. They vary from year to year, and the best authorities in Germany, France and England, to say nothing of America, differ *toto cælo* from each other on some of the most fundamental principles. Some hold that, like the law of gravitation, the laws which govern the growth and decay of language admit of no exceptions; others hold, on the contrary, that disturbances in the regular courses of words may here, lead to the discovery of an unsuspected Neptune. Dialects, according to some, are the descendants of one uniform language; according to others they are the feeders of the classical languages, and exist not only before a common literary language can be framed, but continue to influence its later development by constant intercommunion. Dialect, in fact, has become the general name for the *centrifugal* tendencies of language, whether originating in individuals, families, villages, towns, or provinces, as opposed to the *centripetal* power of analogy, represented by the sway which, whether for good or for evil, majorities always exercise over minorities. But even on minor points there have been most sanguinary battles between hostile camps of comparative philologists. Whether the original Aryan language possessed one short *a* only, like Sanskrit, or whether the *a* was already, before the separation of the Aryan family, differentiated into *a*, *e*, *o*, has been treated as a matter of life and death; and I do not deny that in the eyes of the true scholar it is a matter of life and death. But it does not follow that because Curtius hesitated on this point he therefore deserves all the ignominious epithets that have been showered upon his head. Among scholars by profession all this is understood. Curtius holds, and will hold, his place of honor in the history of Comparative Philology in spite of all that has of late been written against him, and no one will be more ready to admit this, I believe, than Brugmann, Osthoff and others, who have attacked him so fiercely. I am sorry for rude and ungracious language at all times, but I do not mind an honest fight. What I object to is, if critics, who are too lazy to form an opinion for themselves, amuse themselves, and think they can amuse others, by collecting a number of passages from the writings of these philological champions, in which they not only contradict each other flatly, but bandy epithets with which they seem but too familiar, whether from the study of slang dictionaries or from their partiality for the customs of primitive savages. Let every man judge for himself, and give his opinion and his reasons for it; but simply to point out that Bopp has been called an *ignoramus* by somebody—it may be even by some one who is somebody—that Sir William Jones has been dubbed a mere pretender, or Darwin a fool, may no doubt serve to raise a smile, and to bring a whole subject into discredit, but it can do no possible good. What province is there in the whole realm of human knowledge in which there is no difference of opinion? None, I should say, except where there is for a time neither life, nor progress, nor discovery. It is because there is at present intense vitality in the comparative study of ancient languages, traditions, customs, mythologies, and religions that there is in it that constant friction, that frequent scintillation, but also that constant increase of new light. Do you think we shall ever have infallibility and immutability in the republic of learning? I hope not, for to my mind that would mean nothing but sluggishness, languor and death. Scholars welcome everybody who in the open tournament of science will take his chance, dealing blows and receiving or parrying blows; but the man who does not fight himself, but simply stands by to jeer and sneer when two good knights have been unseated in breaking a lance in the cause of truth, does nothing but mischief, and might, indeed, find better and worthier employment.

To say, therefore, that the results of Comparative Philology, Ethnology and Mythology are still too uncertain to make it safe for a philosopher to take them into consideration, is mere laziness. The river of knowledge, like all other rivers, will never stop flowing for timid men to pass through with dry feet; it will flow on *in omne volubilis aevum*, and we must take our header into it, and swim or drown.

There is one advantage at least in getting old. To a young man, or I should rather say to a man of middle age, to see the pendulum swinging from one extreme to the other, to see the views which he learnt with implicit faith from his teacher demolished by men it may be far inferior in knowledge, judgment and character, is often disheartening. But if one is allowed to watch the clock of knowledge for a longer time than is commonly allotted to hardworking students, one feels comforted on seeing the pendulum returning once more to the opposite side, and one finds out that after all there was more to be said for the exploded errors than we imagined thirty years ago.

I say one feels comforted, though others would probably say, "Is, then, our knowledge nothing but a perpetual swing-swang? Must we be content with always oscillating between truth and untruth, and does the flux and reflux of scientific opinion always leave us exactly where we were before?" No; I certainly do not take so desponding a view of our human destiny. On the contrary, I feel convinced that while the pendulum vibrates regularly backward and forward, the finger on the dial—to keep to our metaphor—moves onward, slowly but steadily—unless there is something wrong in the wheels within wheels which represent the incessant toil of honest and unselfish workers.

You may of late years have heard a good deal about new views in Comparative Philology. I highly appreciate every one of these new views, but I do not therefore entirely surrender the old views. There has not been a cataclysm, a complete break between the old and the new, as some giddy people want to make out. There has been, as there ought to be, a constant reform, but there has never been a *coup d'etat.* Some of the very foundations of our science have had to be reexamined, and have been strengthened by new supports. Some important additions have been made with regard to phonetic laws, and on the whole it has been found that many things which were accepted as beyond doubt, were after all not quite so certain as they seemed at first.

Let us only take one instance. You have probably all heard of what I called *Grimm's Law*, and what, as I fully admit, would more correctly have been called *Grimm's Rule.* However, it may be called at least an Empirical Law, for it contains the observation of a uniformity in the changes of consonants in Low German and High German, as compared with all the other languages of the Aryan family. We find the observation of that uniformity in its crudest form in Rask. It was afterward generalized and more firmly established by Grimm. Still, a number of exceptions remained, and these were gradually diminished by the discovery of new rules by Lottner, Grassmann, Verner. But even now, much remains to be done.

There are still exceptions to be accounted for, such as Gothic *fadi*, which as Sanskrit has the accent on the first, ought to be *fathi;* or Gothic *hvathar*, whether, which as Sanskrit *katará* has the accent on the last, should be *hvadar*. Nay, I believe that a higher law has yet to be discovered to account for the influence which, according to Verner, the accent immediately *before* Sanskrit tenues is supposed to exercise. If the accent is on the vowel immediately preceding the tenuis in Sanskrit, the tenuis becomes aspirate in Low German; if not, the Sanskrit tenuis appears in Low German as the corresponding media. Thus Sanskrit *bhrấtar* becomes in Gothic *brôthar*, *t* being replaced by *th;* but Sanskrit *pitár* becomes *fadar;* Sanskrit *mâtár*, Anglo-Saxon *módor*. Why? Simply because the accent in Sanskrit was immediately before the *t* in *bhrấtar*, but not so in *pitár* and *mâtár*. This shows how closely languages are held together, a change of accent in Sanskrit being sufficient to explain the change of *th* and *d* in Gothic, Anglo-Saxon and other Low German dialects.

But we have, as yet, the facts only. Why the accent should exercise this influence we do not know, unless we suppose that the accent before the tenuis draws the tenuis toward the preceding vowel, makes it, as it were, the final of a syllable, and secures to it that aspiration which a tenuis would claim, if the final of a word.*

I wish I could give you to-day a fuller account of the excellent work that has been done during the last twenty years by such men as Lottner, Grassmann, Verner, Ascoli, Fick, Ludwig, Schmidt, Collitz, Brugmann, Osthoff, de Saussure, Schrader, and many others. You would be surprised at the perfection which has been attained in the elaboration of phonetic rules, in the observations on the working of analogy, in the more exact definition of technical terms, and in the historical conclusions to be drawn from the facts supplied by a comparison of cognate languages.

But my object to-day is a different one. I wish to call your attention to the progress that has been made in our comprehension of language itself. Now, whatever views were formerly held about language, everybody was agreed that language was a most wonderful thing, so wonderful, in fact, that perhaps the wisest thing that could be said about it was that it must have been of superhuman or divine origin. It was quite clear that, though men might frame new out of old words, no man could ever frame at his own pleasure a word entirely new. Nor did nature seem to have supplied primitive humanity with a vocabulary,

*See Heyne, *Laut und Flexionslehre*, p. 98; also Sweet, *History of English Sounds*, p. 9.

for all vocabularies differed, and every person capable of speaking had to learn his language from his parents. Whence, therefore, could language, with its millions of words, come to us except from a superhuman and supernatural source? We wonder at the infinite number of stars, and we well may. One look at that silent eternal procession is worth all the miracles of all religions put together. But if the stars on high and the still small voice within seemed to the greatest philosopher the two greatest miracles, might he not have added the galaxy of words as the third great miracle that passes all understanding, though it passes every day before our very eyes? If you consider that the great English dictionary, now being published by the University press at Oxford, is to contain two hundred and fifty thousand words, that is, a quarter of a million, and that on a low average every word admits of at least ten changes by means of declension, conjugation, or degrees of comparison,* you have before you, in English alone, two millions and a half of words, every one a bright star of human thought. I wonder what the number of the stars in Heaven may be. Struve, I am told, formed a guess that their number might amount to two millions! But the visible stars, up to stars of the fifth magnitude, amount

*A Greek verb, according to Curtius, admits of 807 modifications; a Sanskrit verb of 891.

to one thousand three hundred and eighty-two only, and I doubt whether anybody here present has ever seen more than twice that number, as I doubt whether many people have ever used more than twice that number of words. At Oxford, as Professor Pritchard informs me, the stars which we see with the naked eye are about two thousand eight hundred—about the same as the number of the members of the University in their various degrees of light and magnitude.

No doubt English is one of the richest languages, and much of its wealth is kept only in reserve. A poet is very eloquent who uses more than ten thousand words. It is all the more amazing, therefore, to see the intellectual wealth of languages spoken by the lowest savages. Owing chiefly to Darwin's reports, it has been the fashion to represent the inhabitants of Tierra del Fuego as standing on the very lowest rung of the ladder which represents the ascent or descent of man. You remember what Darwin said of them. They seemed to him like the devils which come on the stage in such plays as the *Freischütz*. "Viewing such men," he says, "one can hardly believe that they are fellow creatures, and inhabitants of the same world. Their language, according to our notions," he adds, "scarcely deserves to be called articulate. Captain Cook has compared it to a man clearing his throat; but certainly no European ever cleared his throat with so many hoarse, guttural and clicking sounds!" These Fuegians, as they appeared to Darwin, may be responsible for much that is now called Darwinism. But even with regard to the physical features of these Fuegians, Darwin must either have been very unlucky in the specimens he met, or he cannot have kept himself quite free from prejudice. Captain Parker Snow, in his *Two Years' Cruise off Tierra del Fuego*, speaks of the same race as without the least exaggeration really beautiful representatives of the human race. Professor Virchow, who exhibited a number of Fuegians at Berlin, strongly protested against the supposition that they were by nature an inferior race, or that they might be considered as a connecting link between ape and man. Captain Parker Snow sent me, in 1885, the following interesting letter: "I am now over sixty-seven years old"—that makes him now seventy—"but I would gladly voyage again among those so-called savages, and my wife—same age—coincides. Indeed, we have both lived among wild tribes in various parts of the globe, and never once received aught but kindness and love from them, whether in the Pacific, or Australia, or Tierra del Fuego. Nor from the days when, as a boy in 1834–35, I was much among them, and often since, have I once lifted a weapon to harm them. No occasion. I and mine found them honest, and *above* the ordinary 'civilized' lower strata of life, 'Cannibals' (when from necessity, or revenge, or policy—'to imbibe the white man's powers') though they were."

But what shall we say of their language? The same language which to Darwin's ears seemed hardly articulate is described by Giacomo Bovi, who learnt their language, as consisting of *parole dolci, piacevoli, piene di vocali.* The Yahgan dialect, which has lately been more carefully studied by missionaries, has a dictionary of 32,430 words. Now let us remember that Shakespeare, in the enormous variety of his plays, achieved all he wished to achieve, expressed all he wished to express, with 15,000 words, not quite half the wealth of the language spoken by those devils of the *Freischütz*, whom Darwin could hardly believe to be fellow creatures. Every one of these words represents an intellectual effort, and every one of them can be either declined, conjugated and compounded, according to the strict laws of a most complicated grammar.

I have always had the fullest belief in Darwin's devotion to truth, and I had expressed my conviction that, if the real facts about the language and the general character of the Fuegians were placed before him, he would withdraw the strong language which he had used, after but a short stay among them. And so it was. In a letter, dated

Down, Kent, November 22, 1881, Darwin wrote to Captain Parker Snow:

"DEAR SIR—I hope that you may succeed in publishing a new edition of your *Cruise to Tierra del Fuego*. You saw so much more of the natives than I did, that, wherever we differ, you probably are in the right. Indeed, the success of the missionary establishment there proves that I took a very erroneous view of the nature and capabilities of the Fuegians."

That is what I call real Darwinism—love of truth, not of self or system. It is the heart that makes the true man of science, not the brain only.

What then has the science of language done for us in explaining that stupendous wealth of words and forms, whether in English, or in Sanskrit, or in Hebrew, or in Turkish, or even in the language of the so-called devils of Tierra del Fuego? It has completely changed the aspect of the miracle, and instead of exhibiting language as something incomprehensible, bewildering and supernatural, it has shown us, that the process by which this supposed miracle of language has been wrought is perfectly simple, natural and intelligible. We no longer stare at language in utter bewilderment, but we understand it. Give us the materials, and we can build up a language, perhaps more perfect, though, it may be, less beautiful, than English, Sanskrit or Fuegian.

But what are these materials?

Whatever language we take, we find that it can be analyzed, and as the result of our analysis, we find everywhere *material* and *formal* elements. In *giver* and *gift*, for instance, the material element is *give*, the formal elements are *er* and *t*. In *to wit*, in *witness*, and in *wittingly*, we easily see the permanent material element, *wit*, used in the sense of knowing, and followed by such formal elements as *ness* and *ing*. These material elements are generally called roots, and it stands to reason that in modern languages it is often very difficult to discover the true roots. There have been so many phonetic changes that in order to discover the most primitive form of a root, we must always go back to the more primitive languages. The same root, *wit*, for instance, exists in English in such words also as *history*, but no one who did not know that this word came to us from Rome and Greece, would be able to discover the presence of the root *wit* in *history*. In Greek we know it, because we know that, according to fixed phonetic rules initial *v* is dropt, *d* before *t* is changed to *s*, thus giving us *istor* instead of *vid-tar*, the Sanskrit *vet-tar*.

Now this is one thing which the Science of Language has achieved. It has discovered the material elements or roots in all the Indo-European languages. But while this achievement belongs to the nineteenth century with us, it belonged to the fifth century B. C. in India. In India the earliest grammarians asked the question, which we have asked but lately, namely, What is language made of? and they found, as we have found, that it consisted of those material elements or roots, and of a certain number of formal elements, called suffixes, prefixes and infixes. This was a wonderful achievement, particularly for men whom certain people even now would call savages or niggers. The result of this analysis or taking to pieces of the Sanskrit language is now before us, in a list of about two thousand roots, which is ascribed to the great grammarian Pâ*n*ini, who lived about the same time as Æschylus. Given that number of roots and there is no word in Sanskrit which Hindu grammarians do not undertake to build up. That is to say, the whole flora of the Sanskrit dictionary has been traced back by them to about two thousand seeds. Wonderful as this achievement is, we must not exaggerate. Many of the etymologies of the native Indian scholars are fanciful. The idea that it should be impossible to trace any word back to a root, never entered their heads. If there is no root, a root is invented for any special word, for according to their views, the only object of a root is to account for the existence of a word. Hence many of these roots which we find collected by Pâ*n*ini may be safely set aside. From our point of view, we are quite prepared to admit that Sanskrit, like other languages, may possess words of which the roots can no longer be discovered. We could not discover, for instance, the root of such a word as *history*, if Latin and Greek had been swept away out of existence; nor should we know that the root of *age* was *I*, to go, unless we could follow up historically the traces of that word from *age* to *eage*, *edage*, *ætaticum*, *ætas*, *ævitas*, *ævum*, and Sanskrit *eva*, which comes from the root *I*, to go.

If we sift the list of roots in Sanskrit, retaining such roots only as can be traced in the actual literature, the number of 2,000 dwindles down to about 800. That is to say, with about 800 material elements we can account for the whole verbal harvest of India. Now that harvest is as rich as that of any other of the Aryan languages, and what applies therefore to Sanskrit, applies *mutatis mutandis*, to Greek, Latin and all the other Aryan languages. Their stock in trade is no more than about 800 roots. I should even say, it is considerably less, because as languages grow they drop a number of scarce and isolated words, and supply their wants by new derivatives, or by new metaphorical expressions. I see that Professor Skeat, in his list of the principal Aryan roots occurring in English, brings their number to no more than 461.

Imagine, then, what a difference this makes in

our view of language. We may feel bewildered by a quarter of a million of descendants, but we can manage eight hundred ancestors; and if we can once manage these eight hundred ancestors, their descendants, whatever their number, need no longer perplex and frighten us.

In this respect the Science of Language has brought daylight where all before seemed dark and confused. Whatever in language is not material is formal. These formal elements are in many cases material elements in a metamorphic state. Thus *hood* in *child-hood*, which is now a formal element, used to form collective and abstract nouns, was still not many centuries back, a living word, the Anglo-Saxon *hâd*, meaning state or rank. This *hâd* again is related to the Gothic *haidus*, meaning manner, way; and this *haidus* exists in Sanskrit as *ketú*, a sign. When we have come so far, we ask what is this *ketú*, and we find that its root is *kit*, to observe, to see, while *u* is a purely formal element, used to form nominal and verbal bases in Sanskrit.

Besides these metamorphic words—the soil, as it were, left by a former vegetation—the Aryan languages make use of a number of demonstrative elements, with which to form nouns, adjectives and verbs from roots. These were at first intended to point to whatever was meant to be the subject of a predicative root. If there was a root meaning to strike, then "*strike-here*" might be a striker, a fighter; "strike-there" might be "wound;" "strike it" might be "sword." After a time these demonstrative elements became differentiated and specialized, and they stand now before us as suffixes, and terminations of nouns and verbs.

What has so far been established by the Science of Language is this, that, if we have, say, eight hundred material or predicative roots and a small number of demonstrative elements given us, then, roughly speaking, the riddle of language is solved. We know what language is, what it is made of, and we are thus enabled to admire, not so much its complexity as its translucent simplicity.

There remains, however, the old question, "Whence these roots?" We have found them by careful digging, we have pulled them out of the ground, and there can be no doubt about their reality. There they are, but people want to know how they came to be there; nay, they seem more eager on that point than on the whole subsequent growth of language.

There was a time when the existence of roots was denied altogether, and words were derived straight, either from imitations of the sounds of nature, particularly the cries of birds and the shouts of animals, or from interjections, such as we utter ourselves, whether we like it or not, when under the sway of pleasure or pain, or any other powerful passion. Nothing could sound more plausible. Could the name of the *cuckoo* be anything but the imitation of a bird's note? Could *tolderollol* be anything but a shout of joy? Do we not hear in to *chuckle* the sound of suppressed laughter, and in to *chuck* the clucking of the hen? Now to *chuckle* means also to fondle, so that we can clearly see how so abstract an idea as to caress or to love may be expressed by a sound imitated straight from the cackling of a hen.

And why should not a complete language have been formed by the same process? If *bow-bow* was used for barking, why should it not be used also in the sense of persecuting? If *pooh-pooh* was an expression of disgust, why should it not be accepted as the name of a critical review? And if those who generally *bow-bow* and *pooh-pooh* moderate occasionally the breath of their indignation, or change it into a more or less loud breeze of mutual love and admiration, why should that not be called a *puff*, from which *puffer*, *puffery*, *puffiness*, and all the rest.

All this goes on swimmingly for a short time, but then comes a sudden precipice. There are onomatopœic elements in every language, but they end where real language begins. They are like volcanic rocks breaking here and there through the superincumbent stratified layers of speech. We know perfectly well what they are; they require no explanation whatever; but they are certainly not what we mean by speech, by discourse, or Logos. I had to fight these two theories when I delivered my lectures on language five-and-twenty years ago. In order to describe them by short and clear names I called them the *Bow-bow* and *Pooh-pooh* theories. Description was taken for irony; but whether these names contained truth or irony, certain it is that both these theories are now dead, never to rise again, I hope.

But though so much is gained, and we are not likely to be troubled again with derivations of words direct from the crude sounds of nature, there remains the question to be answered, namely, "What is the origin of those roots which stand like a rampart between the chaos of sounds expressive of mere feelings and the kosmos of words expressive of concepts?"

It is perfectly right to ask that question, but it is also right to see that such a question can admit of an hypothetical answer only. Think of what times we are speaking!—times when no Aryan language did exist, when no verb or noun had yet been formed, when man, in fact, was hardly yet man in the full sense of that word, but only the embryo of a man, without speech, and therefore without reason. We can enter into all the secret workings of the human mind, building up for itself the shell of language, after the materials were once given. But a state of mind without language and without reason is more than we can fully realize. All we can do is to guess, and to guess cautiously.

There are three things that have to be explained in roots, such as we find them:

(1) Their being intelligible not only to the speaker but to all who listen to him;

(2) Their having a definite body of consonants and vowels;

(3) Their expressing general concepts.

In my former lectures I called attention to the fact that everything in nature that is struck vibrates and rings. This is the widest generalization under which the vocal utterances of man can be classed. Under the influence of certain emotions the human body finds relief in more or less musical sounds, produced by the breath passing either slowly or violently from the lungs to the larynx and from the larynx to the mouth.

This is perfectly true; but these sounds which naturally accompany our emotions, though they may supply the material, are very far as yet from being roots. It was Professor Noiré who first pointed out that roots, in order to be intelligible to others, must have been from the very first social sounds—sounds uttered by several people together. They must have been what he calls the *clamor concomitans*, uttered almost involuntarily by a whole gang engaged in a common work. Such sounds are uttered even at present by sailors rowing together, by peasants digging together, by women spinning or sewing together. They are uttered and they are understood. And not only would this *clamor concomitans* be understood by all the members of a community, but on account of its frequent repetition, it would soon assume a more definite form than belongs to the shouts of individuals, which constantly vary, according to circumstances and individual tendencies.

But the most difficult problem still remains. How did these sounds become the signs, not simply of emotions but of concepts? for we must not forget all roots are expressive of concepts. To us nothing seems more natural than a concept. We live in concepts. Everything we name, everything we reason about is conceptual. But how was the first concept formed? that is the question which the Science of Thought has to solve. At present we simply take a number of sensuous intuitions, and after descrying something which they share in common, we assign a name to it, and thus get a concept. For instance, seeing the same color in coal, ink and in a negro, we form the concept of black; or seeing white in milk, snow and chalk, we form the concept of white. In some cases a concept is a mere shadow of a number of percepts, as when we speak of oaks, beeches and firs, as trees.

But suppose we had no such names as black and white, and tree, where would our concept be?

We are speaking, however, of a period in the growth of the human mind when there existed as yet neither names nor concepts, and the question which we have to answer is, how the roots which we have discovered as the elements of language came to have a conceptual meaning. Now the fact is the majority of roots express acts, and mostly acts which men in a primitive state of society are called upon to perform; I mean acts such as digging, plaiting, weaving, striking, throwing, binding, etc. All of these are acts of which those who perform them are *ipso facto* conscious; and as most of these acts were continuous or constantly repeated, we see in the consciousness of these repeated acts the first glimmer of conceptual thought, the first attempt to comprehend *many things as one.* Without any effort of their own the earliest framers of language found the consciousness of their own repeated acts raised into conceptual consciousness, while the sounds by which these acts were accompanied became spontaneously what we now call conceptual roots in every language.

In this manner all the requirements which roots have to fulfill are satisfied. They are necessarily intelligible to a whole community, because they refer to acts performed in common. They have a definite or articulate sound, because they have been repeated so often that all individual or dialectic variety has been eliminated; and they have become conceptual, because they express not a single accidental act, but repeated acts from which all that is purely accidental, temporal or local, has been slowly removed or abstracted.

Professor Noiré, who has most carefully analyzed this primitive process in the formation of conceptual thought, thinks that true conceptual consciousness begins only from the time when men became conscious of results, of facts and not only of acts. The mere consciousness of the acts of digging, striking, binding, does not satisfy him. Only when men perceive the results of their acts—for instance, in the hole dug, in the tree struck down, in the reeds tied together as a mat—did they, according to him, arrive at conceptual thought in language. I do not dispute this, but even if we admitted that the concepts embodied in our roots did not arrive at their full maturity till the acts which they expressed had become realized objectively by their results, we must not forget that every language retains the power of predicating these roots, and that only by that power is it able to produce its wealth of nouns and verbs.

In Sanskrit the number of these roots has been estimated at about eight hundred, and the great bulk of the Sanskrit dictionary has been traced back to these eight hundred living germs. But this is not all. If we examine these eight hundred roots more carefully, we find that they do not represent an equal number of concepts. There are, for instance, about seventeen roots, all meaning to plait, to weave, to sow, to bind, to unite; about thirty roots, all meaning to crush, to pound, to destroy, to waste, to rub, to smooth; about seventeen meaning to cut, to divide, and so on. I believe the original meaning of roots was always special, but became generalized by usage, though, on the other side, certain roots of a general meaning became specialized also. But the important fact which has been established and can no longer be doubted is, that the eight hundred roots which supply our dictionary can be reduced to about one hundred and twenty concepts. These one hundred and twenty concepts are really the rivers that feed the whole ocean of thought and speech. There is no thought that passes through our mind, or that has passed through the minds of the greatest poets and prophets of old, that cannot directly or indirectly be derived from one of these fundamental concepts. This may seem to lower us very much. We thought ourselves so rich, and now we find that our intellectual capital is so small; not more than one hundred and twenty concepts. But does that prove that we are poor? I believe not. Nature has not become poor because we know that the infinite wealth which it displays before our eyes consists of no more than about seventy-two elements, nor is our mind poor because the elements of thought have been reduced to one hundred and twenty, and might, with some effort, be reduced to a smaller number still. What remains to us is the power of combination, of composition and decomposition; and if that power has enabled us to decipher Egyptian hieroglyphics, to determine the metals in the sun, to discover the seventy-two elements of nature, and to elicit the one hundred and twenty elements of thought, we need not be ashamed. Nature produces the greatest effects by the smallest means, and man ought to be proud to follow her example.

THE IDENTITY OF LANGUAGE AND THOUGHT.

Language, under the microscope of the comparative philologist, has turned out to be a very simple thing. With about one hundred and twenty radical concepts and twenty demonstrative elements we could build up a dictionary and a grammar rich enough to supply all the demands of Shakespeare; and surely more than that, no language can fairly be called upon to supply. I stated in my last lecture that, after a careful analysis, I had succeeded in reducing all actual roots of Sanskrit, about eight hundred in number, to one hundred and twenty-one concepts, but I added that the number of concepts might easily have been reduced still further. The fecundity of these roots and the pliancy of our fundamental concepts are perfectly astounding. If you take the concept of uniting, or putting two and two together, you find it expressed by seventeen different roots. No doubt, every one of these roots had originally a more special meaning. Some meant to plait, others to sow, to weave, to bunch, to roll, to tie. But every one of them might have been generalized and afterward again specialized to such an extent that it could have supplied every verb, noun, adjective or adverb expressive of some kind of union; that is to say, one root might, if necessary, have done the work of seventeen.

Now, if I were to take one only of these seventeen roots, all meaning to unite, I am afraid I should spend the whole of my lecture, if I attempted to give you all its derivatives in Sanskrit, Greek, Latin and English. What, however, I wish to make quite clear to you is, that words and concepts, which seem to us quite modern, belong nevertheless to what we should call the very granite of our thoughts. The growth of our thoughts has been historical and continuous. Many of the intermediate links may have been forgotten or lost, but they were there, and it is the object of the Science of Language to restore them, and thus to furnish a safe foundation for the Science of Thought.

We should probably consider *fashionable* a very modern word, and so it is; still it is closely connected with Latin *factio;* and meant originally the make or cut of a garment, whether of a raw skin, as worn by a primitive hunter, or of the most stylish sealskin dolmanette of the present season. We do not imagine that anything could have seemed what we call *queer* to the primitive and sober ancestors of our race. Still, *queer* is only the German *quer*, what runs across, and out of this a name for every kind of oddity or extravagance has been formed. What we call *righteous* was originally conceived as right and straight, straightforward; and the root of right is AR*G*, which means to lead, to steer. From it comes also *rex*, a ruler, a king, *royal* and all the rest. *Gay* is the German *gähe*, literally going, or, as we now say, going it. *Vapid* is like smoke; *rapturous*, from *rapio*, means what carries us away. *Noble*, Latin *nobilis*, from the root GNÂ, to know, meant originally worth knowing, which gives us a high idea of the Roman nobility, at least in its first beginnings. In Kingsley's expression, "one of nature's own noblemen," the original meaning is still faintly perceptible.

What I wish you to see is, that there never was any break in language, that all that is new in it is old, and all that is old in it is new, and that if we take any of the eight hundred primitive roots, or any of the one hundred and twenty simple concepts, we can derive from it any quantity of words to satisfy every fancy of our mind. Take, for instance, the root PA*S*, which in a primitive state of society expressed the act of tethering or snaring.

In Sanskrit this root helps us to express cattle, pa*s*u, which is the Latin *pecus*, Gothic *faihu*, German *vieh*, cattle; also *pecunia* and *pecus*, our lawyer's *fee*. It supplies, besides, pâ*s*a, fetter, and similar words. Now, when we have a word for animal, such as *pecus*, we have also the material for expressing such concepts as *peculiar*, the transition of meaning being clear enough from *peculium*, one's private property, to *peculiaris*, anything that is one's own,—anything that is proper, singular, individual, and, it may be, odd. It is difficult to resist the siren songs of language, and not to follow her into all her flights of imagination. Every word, as soon as we hear it, carries us off to near and distant memories. They float about us like thin gossamer filaments in autumn. But we must for the present resist the temptation of catching at them, and confine our attention to a few only of the principal concepts, expressed by means of our root PA*S*. In Greek, then, this root does not only supply the concept of fastening, but also that of standing fast. Πέπηγα means "I stand fast," and this is a great step beyond "I make fast." We have here the constantly-recurring process of a root, expressive of an act, becoming a root, expressive of a state. Again, what is "made fast" means not only what is compact and solid, but also what is curdled and frozen. Rime, frost, hoar-frost, all are expressed by this root; besides this, the ice, or the scum on the surface of milk,—any raised surface, in fact,—comes to be called πάγος, to which the dictionaries assign the meanings of a mound, a hill, as, for instance, in *Areopagus*, the hill of

Ares at Athens, and the great council held there. What is thick is called from the same root, παχὺς, from which *pachy-dermatous*, or thick-skinned. Lastly, as we say, twofold, from folding, the Greeks said ἅπαξ, once, literally "one stick;" German *Ein-fach*.

If we look to Latin we find an equally large harvest. Here such concepts as settling, agreeing, making peace, are expressed by the root PAS, in *paciscor*, *pactus sum*, in *pâx*, peace, *pacare*, to pacify. This *pacare* helps us to express the idea of *payment*, for to *pay* was originally conceived as to pacify, just as a *quittance* was a quieting. It is so difficult, as I said just now, to resist the temptation of following language through all her vagaries. But when one speaks of *quietus* and giving the *quietus*, and all that, one cannot help thinking of the different shades of meaning which so simple and harmless a word as *quietus* is able to reflect. *Quietus* in English is not only *quiet*, but also *quite*, entirely, as in *quyte* and *clene*, i. e. quietly and cleanly, that is, altogether; while the same word, after passing through French, appears once more as *coy* and *coyish*, a word of a very peculiar flavor, which can only be approximately rendered by quiet, modest, bashful or retired.

But to return to *pâx* and *peace*. We find in Latin a large number of words and derivatives, all springing from the same root. There is *pignus*, a pledge, there is *pâgina*, a page, there is *propâgo*, a layer, then offspring in general; there is also *pâgus*, a settlement, a village, and from it *paganus*, a pagan, a heathen.

In German this root is bifurcated, being either *fah* or *fang*. Thus *fahen* in modern German is to catch, but also *fangen*, from which *gefangen*, captured, *Gefängniss*, prison. *Fähig* means able to clutch, but afterwards *capable*, clever; and *Fähigkeit* is the name for talent. *Fair* also has been traced to Anglo Saxon *faeger*, Gothic *fagr-s*, literally fit, then beautiful, then kind. On the other hand, *finger* seems originally to have meant taker, just as *fang* in English is a tusk or a claw. All these words are only like peaks standing out by themselves, but if we had time we should find every one of them surrounded by greater or smaller heights all leading up to the same summit. The one verb *fangen* enables us to express an infinity of thoughts in German. *Anfangen* means to begin, *Um-fangen* means to embrace, *verfangen* means to catch, from which *verfänglich*, literally perplexing, as *eine verfängliche Frage*, an awkward question. *Empfangen* means to receive, *empfänglich* may express receptive, but also sympathetic, sentimental, and all that. *Unterfangen* is to undertake, but it now has the by-sense of a bold undertaking.

All this is only meant to give you an idea of the enormous variety of thought that can be traced back, and, as a matter of fact, took its rise from one single root such as PA*S*, to tether. Whether we speak of *peculiar* people or of *peace* of mind, of *pagans* or of the *propagation* of the Gospel, of a *page* of writing or of the *Areopagus*, of *Gefängniss*, prison, or of *ein empfängliches Herz*, a susceptible heart, we do it all by means of one and the same primary concept,—PA*S*, to tether.

Multiply that power eight hundred times,—that is to say, take any one of the eight hundred roots and draw from them as Sanskrit, Greek, Latin and German have drawn from that one root PA*S*,—and you will see that a language with such a capital might be as rich as Crœsus.

This may give you a faint idea of what language is and what it is made of, and we are, I think, justified in saying that it represents the simplest miracle in the world.

Let us now turn our eyes on thought. Is thought a very perplexing thing? Is it very complicated, wayward like the wind, tortuous like the convolutions of the brain, inscrutable like the sidereal nebulæ? It seems so. If anything is mysterious, it has often been said, it is our mind; if anything is wonderful, it is our understanding; if anything lifts us above the whole of creation, it is our reason. Even those who use sober and subdued language about everything else, break out into rapturous strains when they speak about the intellect and all that has been achieved by that old wizard.

I shall try to show you that nothing is so easy to be understood as our understanding, nothing so perfectly reasonable as our reason, and that the whole of our intellect, all the tricks of the wizard in our brain, consist in nothing but—addition and subtraction.

This is no new discovery, but it is a discovery that is very apt to be forgotten! One of the cleverest and most consecutive thinkers whom this country or the world has produced—I quote the words of Stuart Mill—declared, more than two hundred years ago, that thinking consisted simply in addition and subtraction.

This may sound very discouraging; but you have only to try the experiment, and you will find that Hobbes was perfectly right. And not only Hobbes, but much more ancient philosophers too. Whoever it was that invented the word *cogito*, knew that to think was to combine, for *cogito* stands for *co-agito* and means to co-agitate, to bring together, to combine; and it is clear that we cannot combine two or many things without at the same time separating them from all the rest.

Whoever found out the word *intellect*, had learnt the same lesson. *Intellect* stands for *inter-lect*, and *inter-lego* meant originally to interlace, to bind together, to combine;—and that is all that the intellect is meant and is able to achieve.

Any book on logic will teach you the same lesson, namely that all our propositions are either *affirmative* or *negative*, that we can do no more than to say A is B, or A is not B. Now in saying A is B, we simply add A to the sum already comprehended under B, while in saying A is not B, we subtract A from the sum that can be comprehended under B.

But why should it be considered as lowering our high status, if what we call thinking turns out to be no more than adding and subtracting? Mathematics in the end consist of nothing but addition and subtraction, and think of the wonderful achievements of a Newton or a Gauss, achievements before which ordinary mortals like myself stand simply aghast. To my mind nothing is more delightful than to see the greatest results achieved by the smallest means, and if our race has completed the work which we most admire, the temple of our intellect, by such natural processes as combining and separating, surely we may be as proud to belong to it as if we belonged to a race of giants.

There is nothing new in all this, it is one of those open secrets which are not often mentioned, but which everybody knows as soon as they are mentioned, though it may be that some people do not like to be reminded of them.

But though the process of thinking, that is of adding and subtracting, is so simple, much depends of course on what we combine or separate. Now what is it that we combine and separate? Most people would answer, we combine and separate what is given us by our senses, and they might say again that nothing can be simpler than what we see or hear, or smell or touch. Whole systems of philosophy have been built upon what is called sensuous experience, and this so-called experience is supposed to be so obvious, so natural, so intelligible, that nothing need be said about it. True philosophy, on the contrary, knows of nothing more difficult, more perplexing, more beyond the reach of all our reasoning powers than what is called experience. Kant's whole philosophy may be said to be founded on the question: "How is experience possible?" Here, too, the stone which other builders refused, is become the head-stone of the corner.

It is curious to see how the senses and what they give us are treated with undisguised contempt by many so-called philosophers. Do we not share our senses with the animals—they seem to say, and is it not, therefore, the lowest kind of knowledge which man possesses? Why trouble about what we can handle and see and hear? Any one can understand that, and there is much higher game for real philosophers. To me it seems, on the contrary, that there is nothing more mysterious than what the senses give us. We can understand our understanding, we can reason out our reason, but we can as little understand what we see and hear, as we can see and hear what we understand. Our sensuous knowledge, so far as its material is concerned, will always remain the standing miracle of our life on earth. So far from despising it as obvious, palpable and plain, we should rather fall down on our knees before it as the unknown, the unknowable, the beyond.

But though this beyond—what Kant calls *das Ding an sich*, must forever remain unknown, we know at least what we have made of it—that is, we know what it has become when we know it. I need not dwell in this place on the well-worn argument that we never can know a thing as it is by itself. To know a thing by itself would mean to know it, not as we know it, but as we *do not* know it, and that is clearly self-contradictory. Then what do we know? We never know things, but we are conscious of our sensations only. We first of all feel pain and pleasure, hot and cold, sweet and bitter, but that is feeling, and not yet knowing. In order to change feeling into knowledge, we must first of all look upon our feelings as caused by something. There is no reason why we should do so, except what we choose to call reason, or what Schopenhauer calls the category of causality. A *tabula rasa*, a wax tablet, simply receives an impression, it does not change it into something that may have caused the impression. The best proof that we are not a *tabula rasa*, as Locke and all sensualistic philosophers imagine, is that we, as soon as we receive an impression, are driven to say, "Something has impressed us." That something, however, is *our* postulate, it is *our* doing; it is simply what *we* create out of the sensations of which alone we are conscious.

But not only do we create this objective world of ours, the things, but we place them, not within us, where the sensations are, but without us, that is, in space. And secondly, we place them without us, not in a lump, but one after another, in succession, or, as we call it, in time. Space and time are necessities of that objective world which we have created, and Kant calls them, therefore, rightly the necessary forms of sensuous intuition.

This may sound very learned, but it is really as simple as child's play. What can we be conscious of? Not anything outside us—for how should we get outside ourselves? but something within us, something that we feel, our sensations. And if we transform what is within us, into something without us, of course it must be *somewhere*—and that is what we call space, and it must be *somewhen*, if we may say so, that is, it must be in time. What is nowhere and nowhen, is, as far as we are concerned, as if it were not. But when we have got so far, when we have changed our sensations into things that are supposed to cause our sensations, and when we have placed them one by the side of another, and one after another, that is in space and time, can we say then that we know them? Let us try the experiment.

I say once more, how sensations arise, how æthereal vibrations produce in us consciousness of something, how neurosis becomes æsthesis, we do not know and never shall know. But having the sensations of light or darkness within us, what do we know of any cause of darkness or any cause of light? Nothing. We simply suffer darkness, or enjoy light, but what makes us suffer and what makes us rejoice, we do not know—till we can express it.

And how do we express it? We may try what we like, we can express it in language only. We may feel dark, but till we have a name for dark and are able to distinguish darkness as what is not light, or light as what is not darkness, we are not in a state of knowledge, we are only in a state of passive stupor.

We often imagine that we can possess and retain, even without language, certain pictures or phantasmata; that, for instance, when lightning has passed before our eyes, the impression remains for some time actually visible, then vanishes more and more, when we shut our eyes, but can be called back by the memory, whenever we please. Yes, we can call it back, but not till we can *call*, that is, till we can name it. In all our mental acts, even in that of mere memory, we must be able to give an account to ourselves of what we do, and how can we do that except in language? Even in a dream we do not know what we see, except we name it, that is, make it knowable to ourselves. Everything else passes by and vanishes unheeded. We either are simply suffering, and in that case we require no language, or we act and react, and in that case we can react on what is given us, by language only. This is really a matter of fact and not of argument. Let any one try the experiment and he will see that we can as little think without words as we can breathe without lungs.

We may say, for instance, that we know the blue sky, or we know that the sky is blue. But how do we know it? Nothing can be blue without us. Outside there may be millions of vibrations of luminous ether, but what we call blue is ours, just as what we call sweet is ours. Sugar is not sweet, *we* are sweet; the sky is not blue, *we* are blue. And who tells us anything about the sky? How do we know that there is a sky and that it is blue? Should we know of a sky if we had no name for it? We have only to try to think of sky without naming it, and we shall find that sky and all that it conveys to us is gone. And so with everything else. If a language has no name for father-in-law, the people who speak it do not know what father-in-law is. They know a person who is the father of their wife, supposing they have names for wife and father, but they do not know any father-in-law. Try to teach a savage what a circle is;—you can only do it by giving him a name. You may point to a wheel;—that will give him the percept or presentation of a wheel. You may give him a rope, fastened to a pole, and making him go round will give him the percept of running round. But the concept of a circle, and more particularly of a perfect circle, cannot be produced or fixed in the mind, except through a name and its definition. It may be said that a geometrician can define a circle without a name, but how does he define it? Again, by means of names. If he calls a circle a figure, he uses a name; if he calls it plane figure, comprehended by a single curve line, he is dealing in names; and even if he called it a mere something, he would still be within the spell of names. We may try what we like, if we want to think, if we want to add and to subtract, we can do it in one way only, namely, by names.

How is it, I have been asked, that people go through the most complicated combinations while playing chess and all this without uttering a single word? Does not that show that thought is possible without words, and, as it were, by mere intuition? It may seem so, if we imagine that speech must always be audible, but we have only to watch ourselves while writing a letter, that is, while speaking to a friend, in order to see that a loud voice is not essential to speech. Besides, by long usage speech has become so abbreviated that, as with mathematical formulas, one sign or letter may comprehend long trains of reasoning. And how can we imagine that we could play chess without language, however silent, however abbreviated, however algebraic? What are king, queen, bishops, knights, castles and pawns, if not names? What are the squares on the chessboard to us, unless they had been conceived and named as being square and neither round nor oblong?

I do not say, however, that king and queen and bishops are *mere names*.

There is no such a thing as a mere name. A name is nothing if it is not a *nomen*, that is, what is known, or that by which we know. *Nomen* was originally *gnomen*, from *gnosco* to know, and was almost the same word as *notio*, a notion.* A mere name is therefore self-contradictory. It means a name which is not a name; but something quite different, namely, a sound, a *flatus vocis*. We

*See note on the etymology of nomen at the end of second lecture.

do not call an empty egg-shell a mere egg, nor a corpse a mere man; then why should we call a name without its true meaning, a mere name?

But if there is no such thing as a mere name, neither is there such a thing as a mere thought or a mere concept. The two are one and inseparable. We may distinguish them as we distinguish the obverse from the reverse of a coin; but to try to separate them would be like trying to separate the convex from the concave surface of a lens. We think in names and in names only.

It is very strange to see how some philosophers are perfectly unable to see the identity of thought and language, while others never doubt it; and still more strange to observe how even those who clearly see that thought is realized and can be realized in language only, yet shrink from drawing the inevitable conclusion, that all philosophy has to deal in the first instance, and in the last instance too, with words, with thought-words, or word-thoughts. It may be both useful and interesting, therefore, to examine some of the leading philosophers as to the opinion which they held and expressed on this subject. Their answers in many cases will turn out to be very different from what one is led to expect from the general tenor of their philosophy.

There is a curious break between the so-called scholastic philosophy of the Middle Ages, and that stream of philosophic thought which, beginning with Descartes (1596–1650), has rolled on without interruption till it has reached the very threshold of this Institution.* That break has had its advantages, but there have been losses also, particularly in the want of precise language and terse argument on the part of our modern philosophers. Hence while scholastic philosophers seldom leave us in doubt as to their views of language and its relation to thought, modern philosophers seem to imagine that they can either neglect altogether that fundamental question of all philosophy, or express themselves in ambiguous terms about it. If we ask, for instance, what Abelard (1079–1142), the disciple of Roscelinus, taught on the relation between language and intellect, he leaves us in no doubt, but states plainly in his own quaint words that "Language is generated by the intellect and generates intellect," thus showing that he had clearly apprehended the interdependence and essential identity of the two.

Hobbes (1588–1679), who among modern philosophers is still most in sympathy with the traditions of Mediæval scholasticism, declares without any hesitation that man has reason because he has language; and he adds, "It is evident that truth and falsity have no place but among such living creatures as use speech."

* These lectures were delivered at the Royal Institution, London.

Locke (1632–1704), though fully aware of the importance of language in all philosophical discussions, could not bring himself to say that thought is either impossible or possible without language. "Most men," he says, "*if not all*, in their thinking and reasoning within themselves, make use of words instead of ideas, at least when the subject of their meditation contains in it complex ideas." This half-hearted opinion we find again and again in philosophers who shrink from the effort of resolute thought. They are ready to admit that it is *almost* impossible to think without words, but where this *almost* begins or where it ends, they never tell us.

Even Leibniz (1646–1716), who may truly be called the founder of the Science of Language, seems rather an unwilling witness to the inseparableness of language and thought. In his "Dialogue on the connexion between things and words," he says, "It troubles me greatly to find that I can never acknowledge, discover or prove any truth except by using in my mind words or other signs." To which his friend answers: "Nay, if these characters were absent, we should never think or reason distinctly."

While Locke and Leibniz were thus constrained, almost against their will, to admit the impossibility of thought without language, Berkeley, their worthy contemporary and rival, was convinced that words were the greatest impediment to thought. He became so angry with language, that in one passage he declared he would in his future inquiries make as little use of language as possible—an Irish bull which was omitted, however, in later editions of his work.

Hume (1711–1776) agrees with Berkeley that we possess no general ideas, but particular ones only, to which a certain term has been annexed which gives them a more extensive signification. But whether these terms had any existence before they were thus annexed, and, what is still more important, whether it is possible to think without these terms, Hume, so far as I can see, never declares in any decisive passage of his works.

It is curious that even Kant (1724–1804) should have said so little on this vital question of all philosophy. He calls language the greatest, but not the only instrument of thought; he admits that without expressions accurately corresponding to their concepts, we cannot become quite intelligible either to ourselves or to others. He declares in one passage that to think is to speak with one's self. But from the very cursory nature of these remarks, we may safely conclude that the problem which occupies us at present, did not excite his special interest, but took its place as part and parcel of the more general problems of his philosophy.

But while Kant thus disappoints us, his townsman, Hamann (1730–1788), a man of wonderful genius, though little known outside Germany, utters no uncertain sound. "Language," he says, "is not only the foundation for the whole faculty of thinking, but the central point also from which proceeds the misunderstanding of reason by herself." And again, "With me the question is not, What is reason? but, What is language? What we want is a Grammar of Reason."

The greatest minds of Germany were all at that time approaching nearer and nearer to the truth, I mean to a perception of the absolute identity of language and reason. Herder (1744–1803) declares his conviction that "without language man could never have come to his reason," and I do not hesitate to add, that, without language man could never have come even to his senses.

William von Humboldt (1767–1835), the greater of a *par nobile fratrum*, wrote: "If we separate intellect and language, such a separation does not exist in reality."

Schleiermacher (1768–1834), the translator of Plato, and at that time the most powerful among liberal-minded German theologians, chimes in with a still clearer note: "Thinking and speaking," he says, "are so entirely one that we can only distinguish them as internal and external, nay even as internal every thought is already a word."

The two most prominent leaders of philosophical thought in the beginning of our century, Schelling and Hegel, divided as they were on many other points, are quite at one on the identity of reason and language. Schelling (1775–1854) says: "Without language it is impossible to conceive philosophical, nay, even any human consciousness." Hegel (1770–1831) proclaims his conviction still more boldly and tersely: "We think in names," he says, as if no one could ever have doubted it.

It may seem a rather violent transition from Hegel to Alphonse Daudet, but in some cases the man of the world, and, we must add, the minute observer of the world, may catch glimpses of truth which either escape the metaphysician altogether, or are at all events not apprehended by him in their realistic fullness. When Daudet wrote his *Roumestan*, it is well known that Gambetta imagined it was aimed at him. He recognized some traits of character in Roumestan which he had discovered in himself, though he imagined that nobody else suspected them. One of them was that Roumestan was unable to think unless he could speak. After a time Gambetta and Daudet met at a dinner given by Hébrard. They sat silent for a time, till at last Gambetta burst out "Where did you get the words which you make Roumestan say, 'if I do not speak, I cannot think.'" Daudet replied, "I invented them." "That is strange," Gambetta replied. The same evening Gambetta and Daudet became reconciled. They seemed to know each other better, and, perhaps, to know themselves better—than many philosophers do.

Of course we must make a distinction. Gambetta felt that he really could not think without speaking, that is to say, without speaking in a loud voice. That was his peculiarity, and it may be a peculiarity common among the people of the South. What Schelling and Hegel meant was not that we cannot think without uttering words, but that we cannot think, even silently, without words. Savages call that kind of thinking, speaking in the stomach, and it would be difficult to find a better name for it.

To return, then, to Schelling and Hegel and their illustrious predecessor, I confess that to myself also it has always seemed incredible that language should ever have been conceived as something that could exist by itself, apart from our whole intellectual nature, or that thought, on the other hand, should have been considered as possible without language. We have only to try the simplest experiment and we shall find that thought, divorced from language, is an utter impossibility. We may see a dog, but if we ask ourselves what it is, if we want to *know* what we see, we can answer by the name "dog" only. Even if we had never seen a dog before, we should still answer by a name only. We should say, it is a quadruped, an animal, or a living thing, a something, but we could do all this by names only, by what the ancients called *Nomina*, i. e. *gnomina*, means of knowledge.

We know, however, what philosophers can achieve, nay, I believe it would not be difficult to show that the sway of philosophical mythology is more powerful even than that of religious mythology. Because we have a name for thought and another for language, therefore, it is argued, there must be thought without language and language without thought. We might argue in the same way that, because we have a name for the outside and another for the inside of a thing, therefore there must be an outside without an inside, and an inside without an outside. We were told at school that the Greeks must have been very strange people, because they had but one word for language and thought, namely, *Logos*, but that they afterward perceived the folly of their ways and distinguished between the Logos ἐνδιάθετος, thought, and the Logos προςορικός, language; as if the ancient Greek conception of language and thought as one, did not show a far greater insight, a far more powerful grasp than the later distinction, useful as it is, between the outside and inside of thought.

However, I can with some effort enter into the

mind of those who, like Berkeley, look upon thought as one thing and on the sounds which we call words as quite another. It is a kind of philosophical hallucination, but there is at all events some method in it. What I cannot understand is, how philosophers can halt between these two opinions, how they can admit that *most* of our thoughts are carried on in language, but not quite all; that *most* people think in words, but not all; that complex arguments may require words, but not simple propositions. What should we say of a mathematician who maintained that for simple addition and subtraction he did not require numbers, but that they were indispensable for higher mathematics. I need hardly say that when I speak of words, I include other signs likewise, such as figures, for instance, or hieroglyphics, or Chinese and Accadian symbols. All I maintain is, that thought cannot exist without signs, and that our most important signs are words.

Among modern English logicians there is a curious lack of courage on this point. The only one who has what is now called the courage of his opinions, is Archbishop Whately. He declares without any reservation that logic is entirely conversant with language. All the rest shake their heads from one horn of the dilemma to the other. Sir William Hamilton deems Whately's opinion too absurd to be imputed to an archbishop. John

Stuart Mill, though in this case less bold than the archbishop, stands up for him so far at least as to try to convince Sir William Hamilton that the formation of concepts and the subsequent process of combining them as arguments, must be considered as a process of language. But Mill himself, in his great work on logic, cannot muster the same courage as Whately. "Reasoning," he says, "the principal subject of logic, takes place *usually* by means of words, and in all complicated cases can take place in no other way." But in what other way it can ever take place, he never shows. He calls language one of the principal elements or helps of thought, but he never mentions any other helps or instruments. He speaks of the reasoning of brutes, but forgets that this is but a metaphorical expression, and that we know nothing of the inside of brutes, except by analogy. He mistakes the abbreviated or silent reasoning of man for reasoning without words, though he would easily have seen that in substituting algebraic or logarithmic signs for the ordinary figures, the mathematician is dealing indirectly with numbers and with numbers only.

The same uncertainty pervades nearly all our hand-books of logic. Archbishop Thomson follows indeed the good example of Archbishop Whately, when he says that we get entangled in absurdities by any theory which assumes that either thought or language existed in a separate state, but he shrinks from drawing the conclusion, that logic deals with language and with language only.

Mr. Jevons cannot bring himself to say that we *never* think without words, but, as a cautious reasoner, he adds, "*Hardly ever* do we think, without the proper words coming into the mind."

Professor Fowler seems inclined to follow Archbishop Whately. "*Practically*," he says, "we always think by means of language;" yet, he adds, "a logician need not come to a decision on this point." Can there be a more vital question for a logician than this? Would any writer on Optics venture to say: "Practically we see with our eyes, but the optician need not make up his mind on this point." Professor Green, a very honest and straightforward thinker, is affected by the same hesitation. "It is hard," he writes, "some say it is impossible, to think without expressing thought in language."

To me it seems inconceivable how any philosopher, that is to say, a student of thought, can leave such a question undecided. I can understand, as I said before, certain minds being so completely under the spell of philosophical mythology as to find it impossible to conceive that thought, which has a name of its own, should not have a separate existence, apart from language.

The ancient nations, because they had called the Unknown by many names, became polytheists, and powerful thinkers only, such as Æschylus, could perceive behind the many names, the one God. But what I cannot understand is how people could be half polytheists and half monotheists, or, as applied to thought, how they could bring themselves to believe that thought, though generally embodied in language, could from time to time walk about as a disembodied ghost. I have myself not the slightest doubt that the time will come when this belief in disembodied thought will be looked upon as one of the strangest hallucinations of the nineteenth century. People do no longer believe in witches, nor in ghosts. But the belief in disembodied thought will die very hard, nay history teaches us that though it was scotched by some of our most powerful thinkers, it always raises its head again and again. If anything can give it its *coup de grâce*, it is the Science of Language, though, strange to say, some of the most popular representatives of that science are against us. Here, as elsewhere, we must have the courage of our opinions. We must make no concessions. We must say "Never," not "Hardly ever," and this "Never," I feel convinced, will mark a new departure in the history of philosophy, nay it will supply a new foundation for every system of philosophy which the world has ever known.

NOTE ON THE ETYMOLOGY OF NOMEN.

Several comparisons of words in Greek, Latin and Sanskrit, which at first seemed so evident as to require hardly any proof, have at a later time become the most perplexing and troublesome. Who would have doubted, fifty years ago, the identity of *deus*, *θεός*, and Sanskrit *dêva*, of *Hêlios* and Sanskrit *Svârya*, of *nômen*, *ὄνομα* and Sanskrit *nâman?* But these are the very comparisons which lately have called forth the largest amount of angry controversy, and to believe in them has almost become a reproach among critical scholars. What my own opinion on the origin and growth of the names for god and sun is, I have stated elsewhere. But, as in my last work on the *Science of Thought*, I have returned to the old and despised etymology of *nomen*, as originally *gnomen*, I gladly state why I consider the arguments advanced against it as non-conclusive.

We must distinguish two classes of objectors—those who deny that any words for name in the Aryan languages have anything to do with the root GNÂ, "to know," and those who are more careful and deny this only with regard to Sanskrit, Greek, German, Slavonic and Celtic, but not with regard to Latin, and would therefore admit two independent words for "name," as they admit two independent words for "god," *deus* and *θεός*.

The first who pointed out the phonetic difficulties which seem to bar the identification of Sanskrit *nâman*, Latin *nômen*, Greek *ὄνομα*, Old Slavonic *imę*, Irish *ainm* (i. e. *enmén*), Gothic *nămo*, was Jacob Grimm. In his German Grammar, ii. 30, in his *Geschichte der Deutschen Sprache*, p. 153, and again in his German Dictionary (1854), he dwells on this subject, and writes:

"It is the custom to trace with great plausibility *nômen* back to the root *dschnâ*, noscere, so that *nômen* would be *gnômen*, 'token, mark,' because we know others by their names. *Agnomen* and *cognomen*, *agnosco*, *cognosco* and *gnarus* speak in favor of it, and instead of *g* we should have prosthetic *o* in *ὄνομα*, Albanian *emeni*, Irish *ainm*. Yet it is a heavy demand to derive even Sanskrit *nâman* from *dschnâ*, *ὄνομα* from *γνῶναι*, Slavonic *imia* from *znati*, our own *namô*, *namo* from *chnâhan*, particularly as the two last named words have the root *niman* and *imjati*, capere, accipere, prehendere, habere, by their side, and *namo* may be conceived as what has been received, attributed, or accepted, while *niman*, Greek *νέμειν*, signifies *capere*, *possidere*, *habitare*. Either *niman* would have to be derived from *dschniman;* or better even, in *nâman*, a transition from the root *dschnâ* to the root *nam*, meaning, in Sanskrit, *inclinare*, *flectere*, would have to be admitted. For such a change of form and meaning there are sufficient analogies."

These protests of Grimm, however, remained unheeded—at all events, so far as Sanskrit, Greek and Latin were concerned. Curtius and Fick retained Bopp's comparison; and I myself pointed out that, at all events, we could not admit two mothers for one child, and that we must decide in favor either of the root NAM or of the root GNÂ.

In 1873 Windisch, in an article on Fick's *Wörterbuch*, published in Kuhn's *Zeitschrift*, could not repress certain qualms of conscience. "I doubt," he writes, "whether *all* the words for name can be traced back to the root *gna*, and have lost their initial *g* in prehistoric times. In Old Slavonic *imę*, we should have to admit loss of *gn*, and Irish *ainm* (for *enmén*) protests by its initial vowel against this etymology, unless we choose to ignore in this case all individual phonetic laws. On the other hand, Latin *nômen* cannot very well be separated from *co-gnômen*. If we are guided by phonetic laws, we must separate at least Latin *nômen* from Old Slavonic *imę* and Irish *ainm*. The Indo-Germanic loss of an initial *g* is likewise a very bold admission, particularly if, in spite of it, the initial *g* is to be made responsible for Greek *οὔνομα*. I therefore suspect the true root of these words to have been *am*. This occurs without any strengthening in Old Slavonic *im-ę*. *O'-νο-μα* shows full nasal insertion. The radical form a-n-m would be preserved in Irish *ainm*, nom. pl. *anm-ann*, and the radical form *nam* in Gothic *namo*, Sanskrit *nâman*. It would not be impossible that in Latin a *g* should have been intentionally added to *nômen*, as *g* was dropt in *nosco*, but retained in *co-gnosco*, *a-gnosco*. The Latin *nômen* has no nearer relation to a postulated fundamental meaning of token."

In 1877 J. Schmidt, in his article on "Metathesis of Nasals" in Kuhn's *Zeitschrift* (xxiii. p. 266), stated the same arguments more fully, and arrived at the four fundamental forms: *anman*, *anaman*, *naman*, *nâman*, without, however, being able to refer them to any root. The first explains, according to him, Irish *ainm*, Armenian *anwan* (for *anman*), Old Slavonic *imę* (from *jenmen*), Old Prussian nom. *emnes*, *emmens*, acc. *emnan* (base *emmna-*), from **enmn-a-*, i. e. fundamental form *anman*, increased be suffix *-a*, like Old Norse *namn*, *nafn*. The second form is meant to explain *ὄνομα*; the third, Gothic *namô*, from *anaman-*; the fourth, Sanskrit *nâman*, Zend *nâman*, Latin *nomen*.

It is curious, however, that after all that can be said on the subject had been said, Grimm's own Dictionary, when it comes to "Name," should give up the derivation from *nëmen*, "to take," because, as the editors (1882) say, the German "*Name*" cannot be separated from Latin *nômen*, which, again, cannot be separated from *gnosco* and root GNÂ. Grimm himself is not responsible for this, nor do the editors of his Dictionary give us any reason to suppose that he changed his opinion—an opinion approved of by Wackernagel also. But Curtius, in the last edition of his *Grundzüge* (1879), is evidently somewhat shaken by the phonetic difficulties pointed out by Grimm, Pott, Windisch and Schmidt; and he leaves it undecided whether we should admit two words for name—one from the root NAM, the other from the root GNÂ, or whether, after all, we may suppose that there were two original dialectic forms of the same word—one *gnâman*, another *naman*.

As to myself, I fully admit that the loss of an initial *g*, or g before n, is totally uncalled for in Sanskrit. If Sanskrit ever possessed the form *gnâman*, it would have retained it as it retained *gnâ*, *gnâ*tas, etc. But the same applies to Greek, which has no objection to an initial γν, and yet possesses by the side of γιγνώσκω other formations, such as νόος and νοέω, which presuppose a root *nâ* or *nu* (*Science of Thought*, p. 621). From such a root *nâ*, Sanskrit might have formed *nâ-man*, Gothic *namô*, Greek ὄνο-μα. We find in Greek ἀ-γνοια, "ignorance," by the side of διά-νοια. Whether Irish *ainm* (nom. plur. *anmann*) and Old Slavonic *i-mę* could be accounted for in this way, I leave to others to determine. But with regard to Latin, I hold that *nômen* was originally *gnômen*, and that the initial *g* was dropt, as in *notus*, *gnotus*, *notio*, while it is always preserved, if medial, as in *i-gnotus*, *co-gnomen*, *co-gnitus*, *a-gnomen*, *i-gnominia*, *ignobilis*, etc. We find the same disappearance of initial *g* in *natus*, *gnatus*, *natura*, *natio*, etc. We must distinguish, therefore, between the Aryan dialectic variety, which would account for a root *nâ* and *nu* by the side of GNÂ, and the peculiar Latin tendency which leads to the dropping of a *g* before *n*, as in *notus*, *natus*, *nodus*, *nixus*, and even before vowels, unless we are prepared to separate *anser* from ha*m*sa and χήν. In the Teutonic languages this tendency is very strong at a later time, as we see in *to know*, *knight*, and likewise in *nut*, *neck*, etc.

Unless, therefore, another root can be pointed out from which to derive such fundamental forms as Schmidt imagines—*anman*, *anaman*,

naman—I hold that Latin *nômen* stands for *gnômen*, and that it meant "name" for the same reason for which Sanskrit sa*m*-*gñâ* means "name." I hold that Sanskrit *nâman* may come from a secondary root NÂ or NU, from which we have Greek *νοῦς*. We ought not to appeal to Pali ña*n*am, "knowledge" for this belongs to a diffierent sphere altogether. If we can thus explain *nâman*, we could also account for Gothic *nămo*, and Greek *ὄνομα*. As to Old Slavonic *imę* and Irish *ainm*, I am quite prepared to wait and see what the most competent students of Slavonic and Celtic phonetics will have to say on the subject. If these words can be traced back to another root, well and good (*Stammbaum* theories fortunately stand no longer in the way); but, if not, this will in no way affect our opinion as to the probable origin of Latin *nômen*, and possibly Sanskrit *nâman*, Greek *ὄνομα*, and Gothic *nămo*. That phonetic difficulties remain, no one would deny. But true scholarship consists in recognizing difficulties, not in trying to suppress them by magisterial assertions, and by dwelling exclusively either on the immutability of phonetic laws or on the absolute necessity of a certain development of meaning. We must weight the one against the other; and in Latin, at all events, *nômen* seems to me, after careful weighing, to incline in the scale towards *gnômen* and root GNÂ, "to know."

F. MAX MÜLLER.

THE SIMPLICITY OF THOUGHT.

If the conclusions at which we arrived in our last lecture are correct—if thought and language are identical, or at all events, inseparable—it would seem to follow that all our knowledge is "merely verbal" or "merely nominal." To most people this will seem a sufficient condemnation of any argument that could lead to so preposterous a conclusion. If we want to express our most supreme contempt for any proposition, we say it consists of mere words. What in our days we are most proud of is that in all our pursuits we deal with facts and not with words. Words, we are told, are the daughters of the earth, things the sons of heaven. A philosophy, therefore, which would attempt to change all our knowledge into mere words, could hardly expect a patient hearing; certainly not in the country of Bacon.

It is difficult to deal with such an objection, because it really conveys no meaning whatever. There must be sense in every word we use in argument, and, as I pointed out before, there is no sense whatever in such an expression as *mere words*. There are no such things as mere words, unless we look for them in those vast cemeteries which we call lexicons or dictionaries. There we find, indeed, mere words, dead words, unmeaning words. The German language, as if to warn us against taking such corpses for living words, calls them *wörter*, and distinguishes them from *worte.* It calls a dictionary a *wörterbuch*, not a *wort-buch.*

Outside a dictionary, however, and outside a madhouse, there are no such things as mere words; nor is there, on the other side, any such thing as mere thought.

Things, it has been well said, are *thinks*, and *thinks* are words. Can we know anything except by means of a word? Is it possible to become conscious of any thought except by means of a name? We may distinguish, no doubt, between names, and concepts, and percepts. But percepts (a term which I use for image or presentation, the German *Vorstellung*), percepts by themselves are nothing, concepts by themselves are nothing, while it is only the three together—percept, concept and name—that constitute what we mean by real knowledge.

Let us try an experiment. It is possible to imagine that people, say some primitive savages, had never seen or heard of *gold.* How would they become acquainted with it? In digging they might receive the impression of something glittering, but even that impression would be of no consequence to them, unless they were startled by it, unless their attention was directed to it; and thus the mere sensation of glittering became changed by them into something that glitters. That change of the subjective sensation into an object of sense is *our work*—it is the first manifestation of the law of causality within us.

But that glittering object is even then nothing to an intelligent observer, unless he can lay hold of it by some concept; that is unless he can name it, unless he can call it glittering. We, at our time of life, find no difficulty in calling a thing glittering, or bright, or shining. We have names and concepts ready-made for everything. But all these names and concepts had first to be made. A number of single percepts of glittering, glimmering, flickering, sparkling, flashing, flaming, gleaming things had first to be comprehended under one general aspect, while at the same time a root had to be found to express it. How these roots were formed I explained in my first lecture. They all owe their origin to the *clamor concomitans* of social acts. Thus glittering goes back to a root GHAR, which meant at first to melt, to fuse by heat. From it gh*ri*ta, liquified butter, or *ghee*. What was melted and liquified by heat was generally not only warm but also shining, so that the same root, in its objective application, came to mean to melt—that is to say, to be in a state of melting, to glitter, to shine. From that root, used in that meaning, we have in English such variously differentiated forms as to glint, to glitter, to glisten, to gleam, to glimmer.

With such a root, then, which was at the same time a concept, it was possible to conceive and name that glittering thing which had been dug up with many other things, and which excited our attention chiefly by this distinguishing feature of being bright. But by being called glitter this dug up thing was not yet gold. Far from it. Its old name in Sanskrit, h i r a *n* y a, said no more than that it glittered, and not everything that glitters is gold. Still, even that first name marks an enormous advance beyond the mere fright excited in an animal by the sight of a flaring object, or beyond the mere human stare, or even the phantasma in our memory. It is knowledge—not much, as yet, but it is knowledge; it is the work of intellect, not the mere passive stupor of the senses.

The same object might be called and conceived by many new names, and with every new name new knowledge would be added. Whatever new qualities a miner discovered as distinguishing this glitter from other kinds of glitter, would be added by means of new names, or new adjectives. By this process what we call the intension of the first name would grow fuller and fuller. But we must remember, every one of these new qualities could be known again by the same process only by which the first quality of glittering was known, namely, by being named. Suppose our primitive savages wanted small stones for building purposes. If among the stones they were breaking they met with some that would not break, they would throw them away, and thus gold might be called rubbish or refuse. If, on the contrary, they looked out for material that would bend and not break on being struck, they would pick out the old glitter which they had thrown away as rubbish, and now call it pliant, flexible, ductile, malleable. All these properties were attended to, known and named at the same moment. Gold was now not only bright, but malleable, and ductile, and by a constant repetition of the process of naming and conceiving, and conceiving and naming, people arrived at last at what we call true knowledge of gold, including its specific gravity, and its power of resisting nitro-muriatic acid, and all the rest. That true knowledge may be more full, more accurate, more concerned with essential qualities than our first knowledge of mere glitter. But there is no difference in kind. Our perfect knowledge is as much nominal or verbal as our imperfect knowledge was, nor can it ever be anything else.

It may be said by those who think it right to despise what they call verbal knowledge, that such knowledge would not help us to distinguish a gold sovereign from a brass penny. But they forget that without a name we should not know either a gold sovereign or a brass penny, much less be able to distinguish them. We may do what we like, we cannot jump out of our skin, and the skin of all our thoughts is language. We begin, no doubt, with sensuous irritation and intuition, but intuition by itself is not knowledge, it is blind; conception by itself is not knowledge, it is empty; a name by itself is not knowledge, it is mere sound. Only the three together represent what we mean by knowledge, and the final embodiment of that knowledge is the word.

If that is so with the names of things which we can touch and handle, it is far more so with the names of objects which we cannot reach with our senses at all. Let us take, for instance, the word *species*. No one has ever seen or handled a species. Even if we should see what used to be meant by species, we should not know it for a species, unless we had first called it so. The first question, therefore, is, How did we ever come into the possession of such a name as species? This is a mere matter of historical research. We know from history that species was a Latin rendering of the Greek εἶδος, and this εἶδος has been adopted in Greek philosophy as a convenient term for distinguishing a lower from a higher class. Thus bulldogs, greyhounds, spaniels, terriers would be called species, that is lower classes or sub-classes, while dog would be considered as a higher class or genus, till we ascend still further and comprehend all dogs, pigs, cows, and horses as a higher genus animal, of which dogs are then a species only.

This, however, was clearly a technical employment of the terms *species* and *genus*, and these names must have existed before, when they had a meaning very different from that assigned to them by the founders of logic. A *genus* meant originally a breed, and was used for any living beings, whether animals or plants, which could be traced back to common ancestors. *Eidos* or *species*, on the contrary, meant originally no more than what is seen, the aspect or appearance or shape of things. These two words were found convenient even during a very primitive phase of thought. Stones that were black or gray or yellow, were considered as different sets or sorts or species. They appeared like each other, but no more. Dogs, on the contrary, that were black or gray or yellow, though if their color alone were considered, they might be treated as sets or sorts or *species*, were conceived as a *genus* or breed, if it could be shown that they belonged to one and the same litter. Thus the two kinds of classification, which seem to us the result of the latest scientific thought, the *genealogical* and the *mor-*

phological, were foreshadowed in the earliest words of our language. In Sanskrit also we have *g*âti, kith, used in the logical sense of genus, while species is expressed by âk*ri*ti, which means form.

Even for logical purposes these two words *genus* and *species* were by no means very appropriate. What was a *genus* from one point of view, became a *species* from another, what was a *species* for one purpose, became a *genus* for another. *Genus* and *sub-genus*, *class* and *sub-class* would therefore have answered the purpose far better.

The very fact, however, that what we from one point of view call a species, may from another point of view be called by us a genus, shows at all events that logical genus and species are of our own making, that we name and conceive them, and that there is no such thing as *genus* or *species*, in the logical acceptation of these words, independent of ourselves.

The confusion, however, became greater still when these two terms were transferred from logic to physical science. What a *genus* was in nature was easy to understand. Individuals descended from common ancestors formed a genus or a breed. In some cases the descent from common ancestors might be doubtful, but the definition of *genus* would not be affected by such scientific doubts.

But what was a *species?* If people had asked that question before they introduced that word into the technical language of physiology, we should have been saved much trouble and vexation of spirit. If different species had, or may have had, common ancestors, they would form together one *genus;* if not, they would form different *genera.* A third is not given, and there is no room therefore for *species* in nature.

We must never forget that what we really have to deal with, what is given us to digest in language and thought, are individuals and nothing else. These individuals either have common ancestors or they have not, at least so far as our knowledge goes. If they have common ancestors, they form one breed; if they have not, they form different breeds. And again I say, where is there room for *species?*

There may be individuals such as man and monkey, of which it may still be doubtful whether they had common ancestors or not. But in that case we have simply to suspend our judgment, and we know that in the end the result can only be, either that they belong to the same breed and in the distant past had common ancestors, or that they had not. There is no room for a third possibility, for which we want the name *species.*

We may speak, no doubt, of more or less permanent varieties, and if we like, we may call them *species.* But varieties are always varieties of one and the same original breed, while species are supposed to be something very different.

If there ever was an Augean stable, it was the stable of species, and to have cleared that stable with their powerful brooms will always be the glory of Darwin and his fellow laborers.

But why did not Darwin go a step further, and with one stroke kill that hydra which unless entirely scotched and annihilated, is sure to put forth fresh heads again and again?

Species is a mere chimera, a myth, that is to say a word made for one purpose and afterward used for another. No one has ever seen a species, and even if such a thing as a species existed, we should not know of it till *we* had conceived and named it as such. If we want to discover the real origin of species, we could only do so by tracing the history of that name and concept from stage to stage back to its first beginnings. That would be a most interesting undertaking, and it would teach us at least this one lesson, that no one has any right to say that species means this and does not mean that. Species means neither more nor less than what different philosophers define it to mean. We often hear disputants laying down the law with great emphasis that such a word means this and nothing else. Who has given them a right to say this? Every word has no doubt a traditional meaning, but traditional meanings, like everything that is traditional, are constantly changing. There is no more in a word than what we put into it, nor can we take more out than we have put into it. Darwin himself often complains of this! "No one," he writes, "has drawn any clear distinction between individual differences and slight varieties, or between more plainly marked varieties and sub-species and species." But why should he not himself have tried to do this? The endless disputes whether or not there are some fifty species of British brambles will no doubt cease after Darwin's researches; but so long as the name of species remains in natural history by the side of genus, individual, and variety, we shall never get out of the real brambles of our language, that is, our thought.

Darwin is evidently under the sway of the old definition that all species were produced by special acts of creation. I have not been able to trace that definition to its responsible author, but surely there is no authority whatever for it. The term species was formed quite independently of any such theological ideas.

The Greeks, when they used *eidos*, or *species*, never thought of Zeus as their originator. Nor do I think that in Germany or France or Italy species ever had that theological odor. Some people seem to imagine that Darwin's great merit consisted in having proved that species were not the result of special acts of creation. I doubt, however, whether Darwin himself would have cared either to prove or to disprove this. What he has proved is, "that the only distinction between species and well-marked varieties is, that the latter are known or believed to be connected at the present day by intermediate gradations, whereas species *were* formerly thus connected." Where, then, is the ground of difference between variety and species, even from Darwin's own point of view, except in our momentary ignorance? What used to be called species, will have to be called either genus, or sub-genus, permanent variety. But there will in future be no room for species in the vocabulary of natural history.

Does not this show how entirely we think in names, and how even the strongest minds are under their spell? If Darwin had asked himself what the true meaning of species was, if he had studied the history of the word, which is after all its best definition, he would have seen that the word has no right to exist in natural history, and his work on the *Origin of Species* would really have marked the end of all species, at least within the realm of nature. A belief in species in natural history is nothing but scientific mythology, and what Darwin calls the search after the undiscovered and undiscoverable essence of the term species, is to my mind no more than the search after the hidden essence of Titans and Centaurs. As soon as we relegate the term species to that sphere of thought to which it properly belongs, the air becomes perfectly clear. We have in nature individuals and genera or breeds; for what we call varieties are no more than the necessary consequence of the accumulated effects of individualization. The slight and almost imperceptible differences which keep individuals apart from each other, which, in fact, enable them to be individuals, may by inheritance become stored and strengthened till they constitute what we call a variety in nature. But these centrifugal forces are always controlled by the centripetal force of nature, and in the end the genus always prevails over all individualizing tendencies.

All difficulties which visit us in the various spheres of thought, whether scientific, historical, philosophical, or religious, vanish as soon as we carefully examine the words in which we think. Let us see clearly what we have put into every word, its so-called intension, and let us never try to take more out of it than we or others have put into it. My wonder is, not that we so often misunderstand ourselves and others, but rather that we ever understand ourselves and others correctly. From our earliest childhood we accept our words on trust. We fill them at random, and when we come to compare and to exchange them, we are surprised if they do not always produce on others the same effect which they produce on ourselves.

And if that is so in treating of the common affairs of life, how much more mischief must language produce, when we deal with philosophical problems? To my mind true philosophy is a constant *katharsis* of our words, and the more thoroughly this process of purification is carried out, the more rapidly the clouds will vanish which now obscure Logic, Physiology, Metaphysics and Ethics. How could there be contradictions in the world, if we ourselves had not produced them? The world itself is clear and simple and right; we ourselves only derange and huddle and muddle it. Hamann said many years ago: "Language is not only the foundation of the whole faculty of thinking, but the central point also from which proceeds the misunderstanding of reason herself." There is, therefore, no help or hope for philosophy except what may come from the science of thought, founded as it is on the science of language.

I can only give a few illustrations, but every one will be able to carry out the same experiment for himself.

How often do we hear it said: "I am not a materialist; still, there is a great deal to be said for materialism." What is the meaning of that? It simply means that we are playing with words, or rather that words are playing with us. If we want to know what materialism is we must first of all study the meaning of the word *matter*. The history of a word, if only we could get at it in all its completeness, is always its best definition. It has been the fashion to laugh at etymologies, but in laughing at etymologies we are only laughing at ourselves. Every word is an historical fact, as much as a pyramid. Now a pyramid may seem a very foolish and ridiculous building, but for all that it represents a real primitive thought executed in stone, just as every word represents a real primitive thought executed in sound. The builders of the pyramids and the architects of our language are so far removed from us that in trying to interpret what they meant by their pyramids or by their words we are apt to go wrong. But the very fact that we are able to tell when our interpretation has been wrong shows that we are competent also to judge when our interpretation is right. The etymological meaning of every word shows us the first intention with which that word was framed, and allows us an insight into the thoughts of those palæozoic people whose language we are still speaking at the present moment. *Moment*, for instance, is not a very ancient word, but how does it come to mean *present time?* *Momentum* stands for *movimentum*, and, being derived from *movere*, it meant motion, and, applied to time, the motion of time. "At the present moment" was therefore intended originally for "at this motion of time," or, it may be, "at this motion of the shadow on the dial." But *moment* had also another meaning. It meant anything that makes move, therefore weight, importance, value. Now if we tried to derive the second meaning from the first, we should go wrong; but we should at once be set right by any one who knew that *momentum* in Latin was used also for the weight which made the scales of a balance move, which was therefore a matter of importance, something decisive, something momentous.

If, then, in the same manner we ask for the original meaning of *matter*, we find that it comes to us through French from Latin *materies*. *Materies* in Latin meant the solid wood of a tree, then timber for building; and it had that meaning because it was derived from the root MÂ, to measure, to make. Wood became and was called *materies* only when it had been measured and properly shaped for building purposes. From meaning the wood with which a house was built it came to mean anything substantial out of which something else had been shaped and fashioned. If people made a wooden idol, they distinguished between the material, the wood, and the form. When statues were made of metal or marble, these also were called the matter or material; and at last, whenever the question came to be asked what anything—what, in fact, the whole world—was made of, the same word was used again and again, till it came to mean what it means with us now, matter, as distinguished from form. This matter, then, which may be wood, or metal, or stone, or at last anything of which something else is supposed to consist, is clearly beyond the reach of the senses. The senses can never give us any information about matter in general, because, as we saw, matter may be either wood, or stone, or metal, or anything else, and such a protean thing escapes entirely the grasp of the senses. We know matter as a name only, but as a name which conveys exactly what we have put into it, neither more nor less.

If that name had been used by philosophers by profession only they might no doubt have differed about the right meaning of the word, but they would have felt bound to give us an exact definition of it. But, unfortunately, philosophy cannot reserve a language for its own purposes. Whatever terms philosophers coin soon enter into the general currency; they are clipped and defaced and recast in the most perplexing way. People now speak of decaying matter, and matters of importance. "What is the matter?" people say, and they answer, "It does not matter."

Such is the injury which words suffer by wear and tear that true philosophers feel it all the more incumbent on themselves to call in, from time to time, the most important words, to weigh and assay them once more, and then to fix once for all the exact meaning which they mean to attach to them. Locke* defined matter as an extended solid substance. I doubt whether we gain much by that definition, for substance comprises no more than matter, while extended and solid means hardly more than that matter exists in space and time. At all events if matter escapes the grasp of our senses, so does substance. To speak of matter and substance as something existing by itself and presented to the senses, is again mere mythology.

Mill evidently felt that substance was nothing substantial but a mere abstraction, that is, a word; and he therefore defined matter as the "permanent possibility of sensation." But that is a mere playing with words. We cannot say matter is possibility, for in doing so we stray from one category into another. We can only say matter is what renders sensation possible, or, more correctly still, matter is what can be perceived, provided that it possesses perceptible qualities. The important feature in Mill's definition of matter is the contrast which he establishes between matter

* *On the Understanding*, IV. 3; p. 420. (Ed. London, 1830.)

and mind, the former being, according to him, the permanent possibility of sensation, i. e., of being perceived; the latter the permanent possibility of feeling, i. e., of perceiving.

If, then, we once define matter as what by its qualities can permanently be felt, in opposition to mind or what can permanently feel, it is clear that in all our reasonings about matter we ought to abide by this definition. What, then, shall we say of a declaration such as we find in Mill's *Logic*, that it is a mere fallacy to say that matter cannot think. He cannot mean a fallacy of the senses, for, as I explained before, matter, as such —that is, matter without its qualities—can never fall under the cognizance of the senses. Matter is a word and concept of our own making, and it contains neither more nor less than we have put into it. But whatever we may put into this thought-word, we must not put into it what is contradictory.

Now I ask, is it not self-contradictory first to define matter as what can be perceived, in opposition to mind, or what perceives, and then to turn round and say that after all matter also may not only perceive, but think? Mill would not venture to say that thought was possible without perception, and therefore his argument that it is a fallacy to say that matter cannot think seems to me a contradiction in terms. I do not say that we could not conceive thought to be annexed to any arrangements of material particles. On the contrary, I should say that our experience never shows us thought except as annexed to some arrangement of material particles. But when we have once separated matter from thought, when we have called matter what is perceived, in opposition to thought or what perceives, we must not eat our own words or swallow our own thoughts by saying that, for all we know, matter may think or mind may be touched and handled.

From this point of view I call materialism no more than a grammatical blunder. It is the substitution of a nominative for an accusative, or of an active for a passive verb. At first we mean by matter what is perceived, not, indeed, by itself, but by its qualities; but in the end it is made to mean the very opposite, namely, what perceives, and is thus supposed to lay hold of and strangle itself. What causes the irritations of our senses is confounded with what receives these irritations; what is perceived with what perceives, what is conceived with what conceives, what is named with the namer. It is admitted on all sides that there never could be such a thing as an object or as matter except when it has been perceived by a subject or a mind. And yet we are asked by materialists to believe that the perceiving subject, or the mind, is really the result of a long continued development of the object or of matter. This is a logical somersault which it seems almost impossible to perform, and yet it has been performed again and again in the history of philosophy.

And do not suppose that I have any prejudice against materialism. To my mind spiritualism commits exactly the same grammatical blunder as materialism. We cannot compare matter and spirit, and say, like the old Gnostics, that one is of the devil and the other of God. Matter is the temple of the spirit. It is immense, it is incomprehensible, it is marvelous. Matter is all that is given us to know, and the whole wisdom of the human race constitutes but a very small portion of what matter is meant to teach us. Why then should we despise matter instead of falling on our knees before it, or at all events listening with the reverential awe to the lessons which the Highest Wisdom has designed to teach us from behind its vail?

There is nothing morally wrong in materialism as a philosophical system. Its weakness arises from the fundamental grammatical blunder on which it is based, the change of *it* into *I*

And the same blunder underlies spiritualism. Spirit was one of the many names by which human ignorance tried to lay hold of the perceiver as distinguished from the perceived. It is a poor name, if you like; it meant originally no more than a puff or whiff, a breeze, a breath. It is an old metaphor, and all metaphors are dangerous things. Still, as long as we know what we mean by it, it can do no harm. Now, whatever definition may be given of spirit by different philosophers, they all agree in this: that spirit is subjective, perceiving, knowing; and if, therefore, spiritualism tried to account for what is objective, perceived or known as spirit, it commits exactly the same grammatical blunder as materialism, it changes I into it.

Matter and spirit are correlative, but they are not interchangeable terms. In the true sense, spirit is a name for the universal subject, matter for the universal object. And as there can be no subject without an object, nor an object without a subject, neither can there be, within a narrower sphere, spirit without matter, nor matter without spirit. Matter is determined by us quite as much as we are determined by matter. As we have made and defined the two words and concepts, matter and spirit, they are now inseparable; and the two systems of philosophy, materialism and spiritualism, have no sense by themselves but will have to be merged in the higher system of idealism. The science of language teaches us what such words as matter and spirit meant in the beginning, and what they came to mean in course of time in different schools of philosophy. The science of thought has to teach us what such words shall or shall not mean in future; nay, it has sometimes to relegate them altogether from the dictionary of philosophy.

These few illustrations must suffice to show you what work the science of thought has to do. It has to carry out a complete reformation of all philosophy, and it has to do this by examining the foundations on which philosophy stands, by analyzing every brick with which its walls have been built, by testing all the arches on which its cupola is made to rest. If we think in words we must never take words on trust, but must be ready to give an account of every term with which our thinking and speaking is carried on.

I showed how in natural history the one term *species*, which was introduced at random we hardly know by whom, has caused endless confusion of thought. As there was the term species, it was taken for granted that there must be something corresponding to it in nature. Now I have nothing to say against species in the Aristotelian sense of the word. It is a useful word for many purposes, as when we have to speak of swords, or knives, or books, or any other sort of things as so many species. But in nature there is no need and no room for species, and to try to find the origin of species in nature is like trying to find the origin of ghosts and goblins. The science of thought is meant to break the spell of words, but that spell is far more powerful than we imagine.

One of the richest sources of philosophical mythology springs from the transition of nouns of quality into nouns of substance. We are quite correct, for instance, in saying I feel hungry, or, I am hungry and thirsty, and we may safely speak of our hunger or thirst if we restrict these words to the expression of qualities or states. But when language leads us on to say, I have hunger, I have thirst, hunger and thirst are apt to become entities. We then go on to say that we are driven by hunger or thirst, or that we have lost our hunger and thirst, that is, our appetite. And then the question arises, What is hunger and thirst, or what are our appetites, our desires, our passions? We imagine that we possess something which we may call our passions. We ask for their seat, for their origin, for their nature, and then the psychologist steps in and dissects these passions, and describes them as if they were things or entities by themselves, like corpses on a dissecting table.

In this case, however, a little reflection suffices to show us that to speak of passions and appetites by themselves is only a convenient way of speaking, and no one would think that he was being robbed if passions are shown to be no more than states of feeling.

It is different, however, when the science of thought proceeds to show by exactly the same analysis that there is no such thing as intellect, understanding and reason. "I reason" meant, as we saw, "I add and subtract." If, then, we proceed to say that we possess reason, that means no more than that we possess addition and subtraction. No one, however, would say that, because we can combine, or add and subtract, therefore there is some entity, or faculty, or power, or force within us called combination, which enlightens us, which lifts us above the animal creation, which rules our thoughts—nay, which governs the whole world. I do not deny that we reason; on the contrary, I hold that we do nothing else. But as little as we possess a thing called hunger because we are hungry, or a thing called patience because we are patient, do we possess a thing called reason because we are rational. Why, then, should philosophers trouble their heads about the true seat of reason, whether it is in the brain or in the heart or in the stomach? Why should they write it with a capital R, and make a goddess of Reason and worship her, as she was actually worshiped in the streets of Paris? What would the French mob have said if they had been told that in worshiping this goddess of Reason they were worshiping addition and subtraction? Yet so it was; and possibly addition and subtraction were something far more perfect and wonderful than the goddess of Reason before whom they knelt and burnt incense.

This is, of course, an extreme case of philosophical mythology and idolatry, but the number of these psychological gods and goddesses, heroes, fairies and hobgoblins is very large. Our mind is swarming with them, and every one of them counts a number of worshipers who are deeply offended if we doubt their existence. The protests are already beginning, as I fully anticipated, against my philosophical heresy in having denied the existence of reason, intellect and understanding. As the Ephesians cried out with one voice about the space of two hours, "Great is Diana of the Ephesians!" I know I shall have to hear for the space of more than two hours, the shout of my critics, "Great is the Reason, great is the Intellect, great is the Understanding of the Reviewers!" Yet I am not a blasphemer of the great goddess of Reason; all I have tried to show is that to reason—that is, to add and to subtract—is simply an act which we perform, and that the goddess, if goddess there must be, is not an image which fell down from Jupiter, but the voice within us which makes us keep a true account of all we think and speak and do.

It is difficult—nay, it is impossible—to give in a course of three lectures an adequate idea of what

I mean by the science of thought, still more to answer all the more or less obvious objections that may be raised against the fundamental principle of that science, namely, the identity of thought and language. I must ask you to look upon these three lectures as a kind of a preface only; and if you think the subject worthy of a fuller consideration, this large volume on the *Science of Thought* which I have just published will give you all the necessary material, and will supply the answers to many of the questions which have been addressed to me by some of those who have done me the honor of attending these lectures. One of the questions which I have been asked most frequently is: If thought is identical with language, what about deaf and dumb people? Are they unable to think because they are unable to speak?

My answer is, first of all, that deaf and dumb people are exceptions, and we must not allow our general arguments to be influenced by a few anomalies. Secondly, I have the authority of the best judges, such as Professor Huxley, for stating that a man born dumb, notwithstanding his great cerebral mass and his inheritance of strong intellectual instincts, would be capable of few higher intellectual manifestations than an orang or a chimpanzee if he were confined to the society of dumb associates. Thirdly, we must remember that words are not the only embodiment of thought. Holding up three fingers is as good a sign for the addition of one, one, one, as the sound of three. Shaking the fist in the face is as expressive as saying "Don't." Hieroglyphic writing shows us how our thoughts may be embodied in signs without any reference to the sound of spoken words, and Chinese is read and understood perfectly by people who, when they pronounce and speak it, are quite unintelligible to each other.

It is by means of signs appealing to the sense of sight, and not at first to the sense of hearing, that deaf and dumb people are educated and thus become what they were meant to be, rational beings.

Again, as to animals, I have been asked whether they, because they are dumb, must be declared to be incapable of thought. Here the science of thought steps in at once and says: "Before you ask whether animals think, define what you mean by thinking." Descartes, in his famous aphorism which is supposed to form the foundation of all modern philosophy, *Cogito, ergo sum*, explains *cogito*, I think, as comprising every kind of mental action. If, therefore, we mean by thinking, perceiving, enjoying, remembering, fearing, loving, and all the rest, we have no grounds for denying animals, particularly the higher animals, the possession of these qualities. Their enjoyments, their fears and hopes, their loves and disappointments may be different from ours, still, with the usual discount, animals may claim for the troubles of their souls the same words which we use for our own. Every philosopher, however, knows that what we seem to know of the inner workings of the mind of animals we cannot know directly, but by analogy only. We judge by signs. If, then, we mean by thought that mental function which has its outward sign and embodiment in language, we must say that animals do not think as we think, namely, in words. They may think in their own way. Their way of thinking may be, for all we know, more perfect than our own. I am inclined to believe all the good that can possibly be said of animals, but I cannot allow that they think, if we define thinking by speaking.

Definition, here as elsewhere, is the only salvation of philosophy. If we wish to fight and conquer we must look to our swords; if we wish to argue and to conquer we must look to our words. "Looking to our words" is the fundamental lesson of the science of thought. Do not let us despise words. They are the most wonderful things in the world. Their history, or, as we now call it, their evolution, is more surprising than evolution in any other sphere of nature. The beginnings are so few and so small, their final outcome so magnificent and overwhelming. To some minds, I know, nothing seems grand or worthy of admiration except what is intricate, complex and almost unintelligible; to others there is nothing more fascinating than what is simple, regular and almost transparent. The science of thought appeals to the latter class. And as Kant, when in his *Critique of Reason* he had disentangled the skein of mediæval philosophy, exclaimed in the words of Persius: "*Tecum habita et noris quam sit tibi curta supellex!*" we may sum up the result of the science of thought in the same words: "Dwell with thyself and you will know how small thy household is!"

APPENDIX.

THOUGHT WITHOUT WORDS.

The following correspondence between Mr. F. Galton, Mr. George Romanes, the Duke of Argyll, etc., and Professor Max Müller on "Thought Without Words," is reprinted from *Nature* after careful revision:

I. LETTER FROM MR. F. GALTON, F.R.S.

May 12, 1887.

The recent work of Prof. Max Müller contains theories on the descent of man which are entirely based on the assertion that not even the most rudimentary processes of true thought can be carried on without words. From this he argues that as man is the only truly speaking animal the constitution of his mind is separated from that of brutes by a wide gulf, which no process of evolution that advanced by small steps could possibly stride over. Now, if a single instance can be substantiated of a man thinking without words, all this anthropological theory, which includes the more ambitious part of his work, will necessarily collapse.

I maintain that such instances exist, and the first that I shall mention, and which I will describe, at length, is my own. Let me say that I am accustomed to introspection, and have practised it seriously, and that what I state now is not random talk but the result of frequent observation. It happens that I take pleasure in mechanical contrivances; the simpler of these are thought out by me absolutely without the use of any mental words. Suppose something does not fit; I examine it, go to my tools, pick out the right ones, and set to work and repair the defect, often without a single word crossing my mind. I can easily go through such a process in imagination, and inhibit any mental word from presenting itself. It is well known at billiards that some persons play much more "with their heads" than others. I am but an indifferent player; still, when I do play, I think out the best stroke as well as I can, but not in words. I hold the cue with nascent and anticipatory gesture, and follow the probable course of the ball from cushion to cushion with my eye before I make the stroke, but I say nothing whatever to myself. At chess, which I also play indifferently, I usually calculate my moves, but not more than one or two stages ahead, by eye alone.

Formerly, I practised fencing, in which, as in billiards, the "head" counts for much. Though I do not fence now, I can mentally place myself in a fencing position, and then I am intent and mentally mute. I do not see how I could have used mental words, because they take me as long to form as it does to speak or to hear them, and much longer than it takes to read them by eye (which I never do in imagination). There is no time in fencing for such a process. Again, I have many recollections of scrambles in wild places, one of which is still vivid, of crossing a broad torrent from stone to stone, over some of which the angry-looking water was washing. I was intellectually wearied when I got to the other side, from the constant care and intentness with which it had been necessary to exercise the judgment. During the crossing, I am sure, for similar reasons to those already given, that I was mentally mute. It may be objected that no true thought is exercised in the act of picking one's way, as a goat could do that, and much better than a man. I grant this as regards the goat, but deny the inference, because picking the way under difficult conditions does, I am convinced, greatly strain the attention and judgment. In simple algebra, I never used mental words. Latterly, for example, I had some common arithmetic series to sum, and worked them out not by the use of the formula, but by the process through which the formula is calculated, and that without the necessity of any mental word. Let us suppose the question was, how many strokes were struck by a clock in twelve hours (not counting the half-hours), then I should have written 1, 2 . . .; and below it, 12, 11, . . .; then 2 . . . . 13×12, then $13 \times 6 = 78$. Addition, as De Morgan somewhere insisted, is far more swiftly done by the eye alone; the tendency to use mental words should be withstood. In simple geometry I always work with actual or mental lines; in fact, I fail to arrive at the full conviction that a problem is fairly taken in by me, unless I have contrived somehow to disembarrass it of words.

Prof. Max Müller says that no one can think of a dog without mentally using the word dog, or its equivalent in some other language, and he offers this as a crucial test of the truth of his theory. It utterly fails with me. On thinking of a dog, the name at once disappears, and I find myself mentally in that same expectant attitude in which I should be if I were told that a dog was in an obscure part of the room or just coming round the corner. I have no clear visual image of a dog, but the sense of an ill-defined spot that might shape itself into any specified form of dog, and that might jump, fawn, snarl, bark, or do anything else that a dog might do, but nothing else. I address myself in preparation for any act of the sort, just as when standing before an antagonist in fencing I am ready to meet any thrust or feint, but exclude from my anticipation every movement that falls without the province of fair fencing.

He gives another test of a more advanced mental process, namely, that of thinking of the phrase "*cogito, ergo sum*," without words. I addressed myself to the task at a time when I was not in a mood for introspection, and was bungling over it when I insensibly lapsed into thinking, not for the first time, whether the statement was true. After a little, I surprised myself hard at thought in my usual way—that is, without a word passing through my mind. I was alternately placing myself mentally in the attitude of thinking, and then in that of being, and of watching how much was common to the two processes.

It is a serious drawback to me in writing, and still more in explaining myself, that I do not so easily think in words as otherwise. It often happens that after being hard at work, and having arrived at results that are perfectly clear and satisfactory to myself, when I try to express them in language I feel that I must begin by putting myself upon quite another intellectual plane. I have to translate my thoughts into a language that does not run very evenly with them. I therefore waste a vast deal of time in seeking for appropriate words and phrases, and am conscious, when required to speak on a sudden, of being often very obscure through mere verbal maladroitness, and not through want of clearness of perception. This is one of the small annoyances of my life. I may add that often while engaged in thinking out something I catch an accompaniment of nonsense words, just as the notes of a song might accompany thought. Also, that *after* I have made a mental step, the appropriate word frequently follows as an echo; as a rule, it does not accompany it.

Lastly, I frequently employ nonsense words as temporary symbols, as the logical *x* and *y* of ordinary thought, which is a practice that, as may well be conceived, does not conduce to clearness of exposition. So much for my own experiences, which I hold to be fatal to that claim of an invariable dependence between thoughts and words which Prof. Max Müller postulates as the ground of his anthopological theories.

As regards the habits of others, at the time when I was inquiring into the statistics of mental imagery, I obtained some answers to the following effect: "I depend so much upon mental pictures that I think if I were to lose the power of seeing them I should not be able to think at all." There is an admirable little book published last year or the year before by Binet, *Sur le Raisonnement*, which is clear and solid, and deserves careful reading two or three times over. It contains pathological cases in which the very contingency of losing the power of seeing mental pictures just alluded to has taken place. The book shows the important part played by visual and motile as well as audile, imaginations in the act of reasoning. This and much recent literature on the subject seems wholly unknown by Prof. Max Müller, who has fallen into the common error of writers not long since, but which I hoped had now become obsolete, of believing that the minds of every one else are like one's own. His aptitudes and linguistic pursuits are likely to render him peculiarly dependent on words, and the other literary philosophers whom he quotes in partial confirmation of his extreme views are likely for the same cause, but in a less degree, to have been similarly dependent. Before a just knowledge can be attained concerning any faculty of the human race we must inquire into its distribution among all sorts and conditions of men, and on a large scale, and not among those persons alone who belong to a highly specialized literary class.

I have inquired myself so far as opportunities admitted, and arrived at a result that contradicts the fundamental proposition in the book before us, having ascertained, to my own satisfaction at least, that in a relatively small number of persons true thought is habitually carried on without the use of mental or spoken words.

FRANCIS GALTON.

II. LETTER FROM THE DUKE OF ARGYLL.

ARGYLL LODGE, KENSINGTON, May 12, 1887.

I do not see that Prof. Max Müller's theory of the inseparability of thought from language, whether true or erroneous, has any important bearing on the origin of man, whether by evolution or otherwise. It is a question at all events to be studied by itself, and to be tested by such experiments as we can make by introspection, or by such facts as can be ascertained by outward observation.

My own opinion is strongly in favor of the conclusion urged by Mr. F. Galton. It seems to me quite certain that we can and do constantly think of things without thinking of any sound, or word, as designating them. Language seems to me to be necessary to the *progress of thought*, but not at all necessary to the mere *act of thinking*. It is a product of thought; an expression of it; a vehicle for the communication of it; a channel for the conveyance of it; and an embodiment which is essential to its growth and continuity. But it seems to me to be altogether erroneous to represent it as any inseparable part of cogitation. Monkeys and dogs are without true thought not because they are speechless; but they are speechless because they have no abstract ideas, and no true reasoning powers. In parrots the power of mere articulation exists sometimes in wonderful perfection. But parrots are no cleverer than many other birds which have no such power.

Man's vocal organs are correlated with his brain. Both are equally mysterious because they are co-operative, and yet separable, parts of one "plan." ARGYLL.

III. LETTER FROM MR. HYDE CLARKE.

32 ST. GEORGE'S SQUARE, S. W., May 12, 1887.

Having much of the same experience as Mr. Galton, I nevertheless prefer dealing with a larger group of facts. I have often referred to the mutes of the seraglio at Constantinople, who cannot be charged with thinking in words. They have their own sign conversation among themselves, and which has no necessary reference to words. Even the names of individuals are suppressed among themselves, though they sometimes use lip reading to an outsider to make him understand a name. Any one having a knowledge of sign language is aware that it is independent of words. The tenses of verbs, etc., are supplied by gestures.

The mutes are not deficient in intelligence. They take a great interest in politics, and have the earliest news. It is true this is obtained by hearing, though they are supposed to be deaf-mutes, but among themselves everything is transmitted by signs.

HYDE CLARKE.

IV. LETTER FROM MR. T. MELLARD READE.

I think that all who are engaged in mechanical work and planning will fully indorse what Mr. Francis Galton says as to thought being unaccompanied by words in the mental processes gone through. Having been all my life since school-days engaged in the practice of architecture and civil engineering, I can assure Prof. Max Müller that designing and invention are done entirely by mental pictures. It is, I find, the same with original geological thought—words are only an incumbrance. For the conveyance and accumulation of knowledge some sort of symbols is required, but it appears to me that spoken language or written words are not absolutely necessary, as other means of representing ideas could be contrived. In fact, words are in many cases so cumbersome that other methods *have* been devised for imparting knowledge. In mechanics the graphic method, for instance.

T. Mellard Reade.

V. LETTER FROM S. F. M. Q.

On reading Mr. Galton's letter, I cannot help asking how Prof. Max Müller would account for early processes of thought in a deaf-mute: does he deny them? S. F. M. Q.

VI. LETTER FROM PROF. MAX MÜLLER.

All Souls' College, Oxford, May 15, 1887.

Dear Mr. Galton—I have to thank you for sending me the letter which you published in *Nature*, and in which you discuss the fundamental principle of my recent book on the *Science of Thought*, the identity of language and reason. Yours is the kind of criticism I like—honest, straightforward, to the point. I shall try to answer your criticism in the same spirit.

You say, and you say rightly, that if a single instance could be produced of a man reasoning without words, my whole system of philosophy would collapse; and you go on to say that you yourself are such an instance—that you can reason without words.

So can I, and I have said so in several passages of my book. But what I call reasoning without words is no more than reasoning without pronouncing words. With you it seems to mean reasoning without possessing words. What I call, with Leibniz, symbolic, abbreviated, or hushed language, what savages call "speaking in the stomach," presupposes the former existence of words. What you call thinking without words seems to be intended for the thinking of beings, whether men or animals, that possess as yet no words for what they are thinking.

Now let us try to understand one another—that is to say, let us define the words we are using. We both use thinking in the sense of reasoning. But thinking has been used by Descartes and other philosophers in a much wider sense also, so as to include sensation, passions and intuitive judgments, which clearly require no words for their realization. It is necessary, therefore, to define what we mean by thinking before we try to find out whether we can think without words. In my book on the *Science of Thought* I define thinking as addition and subtraction. That definition may be right or wrong, but every writer has the right—nay, the duty, I should say—to explain in what sense he intends to use certain technical terms. Though nowadays this is considered rather pedantic, I performed that duty on the very first page of my book, and it seems somewhat strange that a reviewer in the *Academy* should accuse me of not having defined what I mean by thinking, for most reviewers look at least at the first page of a work which is given them to review.

Now, the cases which you mention of wordless thought are not thought at all in my sense of the word. I grant that animals do a great deal of work by intuition, and that we do the same—nay, that we often do that kind of work far more quickly and far more perfectly than by reasoning. You say, for instance, that you take pleasure in mechanical contrivances, and if something does not fit you examine it, go to your tools, pick out the right one, set to work and repair the defect often without a single word crossing your mind. No doubt you can do that. So can the beaver and the bee. But neither the beaver nor the bee would say what you say, namely, that in doing this "*you inhibit any mental word from presenting itself.*" What does that mean if not that the mental words are there, the most complicated thought-words, such as *tool*, *defect*, *fit*, are there? only you do not pronounce them, as little as you pronounce "two shillings and sixpence" when you pay a cabman half-a-crown.

The same applies to what you say about billiards and fencing. Neither cannoning nor fencing is thinking. The serpent coiling itself and springing forward and shooting out its fangs does neither think nor speak. It sees, it feels, it acts; and, as I stated on p. 8 of my book, that kind of instantaneous and thoughtless action is often far more successful than the slow results of reasoning. Well do I remember when I was passing through my drill as a volunteer, and sometimes had to think what was right and what was left, being told by our sergeant, "Them gentlemen as thinks will never do any good." I am not sure that what we call genius may not often be a manifestation of our purely animal nature—a sudden tiger's spring rather than *une longue patience.*

It is different, however, with chess. A chess-player may be very silent, but he deals all the time with thought-words or word-thoughts. How could it be otherwise? What would be the use of all his foresight, of all his intuitive combination, if he did not manipulate with king, queen, knights and castles? and what are all these but names, most artificial names, too, real agglomerates of ever so many carefully embedded facts or observations?

An animal may build like the beaver, shoot like the serpent, fence like the cat, climb like the goat; but no animal can play chess, and why? Because it has no words, and therefore no thoughts for what we call king, queen and knights, names and concepts which we combine and separate according to their contents—that is, according to what we ourselves or our ancestors have put into them.

You say, again, that in algebra, the most complicated phase of thought, we do not use words. Nay, you go on to say that in algebra "*the tendency to use mental words should be withstood.*" No doubt it should. The player on the pianoforte should likewise withstand the tendency of saying, now comes C, now comes D, now comes E, before touching the keys. But how could there be a tendency to use words, or, as you say in another place, "*to disembarrass ourselves of words,*" if the words were not there? In algebra we are dealing not only with words but with words of words, and it is the highest excellence of language if it can thus abbreviate itself more and more. If we had to pronounce every word we are thinking our progress would be extremely slow. As it is, we can go through a whole train of thought without uttering a single word, because we have signs not only for single thoughts but for whole chains of thought. And yet, if we watch ourselves, it is very curious that we can often feel the vocal chords and the muscles of the mouth moving as if we were speaking; nay, we know that during efforts of intense thought a word will sometimes break out against our will; it may be, as you say, a nonsense word, yet a word which for some reason or other could not be inhibited from presenting itself.

You say you have sometimes great difficulty in finding appropriate words for your thoughts: Who has not? But does that prove that thoughts can exist without words? Quite the contrary. Thoughts for which we cannot find appropriate words are thoughts expressed as yet by inappropriate, very often by very general, words. You see a thing and you do not know what it is, and therefore are at a loss how to call it. There are people who call everything "that thing"—in French "*chose*"—because they are lazy thinkers and, therefore, clumsy speakers. But even "thing" and "*chose*" are names. The more we distinguish, the better we can name. A good speaker and thinker will not say "that thing," "that person," "that man," "that soldier," "that officer," but he will say at once "that lieutenant-general of fusiliers." He can name appropriately because he knows correctly, but he knows nothing correctly or vaguely except in a string of names from officer down to thing. Embryonic thought which never comes to the birth is not thought at all, but only the material out of which thought may spring. Nor can infant thought, which cannot speak as yet, be called living thought, though the promise of thought is in it. The true life of thought begins when it is named, and has been received by baptism into the congregation of living words.

You say that "after you have made a mental step the appropriate word frequently follows as an echo; as a rule, it does not accompany it." I know very well what you mean. But only ask yourself what mental step you have made and you will see you stand on words; more or less perfect and appropriate, true; but nevertheless, always words. You blame me for having ignored your labors, which were intended to show that the minds of every one are not like one's own. You know that I took a great deal of interest in your researches. They represented to me what I should venture to call the dialectology of thought. But dialects of thought do not affect the fundamental principles of thinking; and the identity of language and reason can hardly be treated as a matter of idiosyncrasy.

You also blame me for not having read a recent book by Monsieur Binet. Dear Mr. Galton, as I grow older I find it the most difficult problem in the world what new books we may safely leave unread. Think of the number of old books which it is not safe to leave unread; and yet, when I tell my friends that in order to speak the *lingua franca* of philosophy they ought, at least, to read Kant, they shrug their shoulders and say they have no time, or, *horribile dictu*, that Kant is obsolete. I have, however, ordered Binet, and shall hereafter quote him as an authority. But who is an authority in these days of anarchy? I quoted the two greatest authorities in Germany and England in support of my statement that the genealogical descent of man from any other known animal was as yet *unproven*, and I am told by my reviewer in the *Academy* that such statements "deserve to be passed over in respectful silence." If such descent were proved it would make no difference whatever to the science of thought. Man would remain to me what he always has been, the perfect animal; the animal would remain the stunted man. But why waste our thoughts on things that may be or may not be? One fact remains, animals have no language. If, then, man cannot think—or, better, cannot reason—without language, I think we are right in contending that animals do not reason as man reasons, though for all we know they may be all the better for it. Yours very truly,

Francis Galton, Esq., F.R.S. F. MAX MÜLLER.

VII. LETTER FROM MR. F. GALTON, F.R.S.

42 RUTLAND GATE, S. W., May 18, 1887.

DEAR PROFESSOR—Thank you much for your full letter. I have not yet sent it on to *Nature* because it would have been too late for this week's issue, and more especially because I thought you might like to reserve your reply, not only until you had seen my own answer to what you have said in it, but also until others should have written, and possibly also until you had looked at Binet, and some of the writers he quotes. So I send you very briefly my answer, but the letter shall go to *Nature* if you send me a post-card to send it.

In my reply, or in any future amplification of what is already written, I should emphasize what was said about fencing, etc., *with the head*, distinguishing it from intuitive actions (due, as I and others hold, to inherited or personal habit).

The inhibition of words in the cases mentioned was, I should explain, analogous to this:—There are streets improvements in progress hereabouts. I set myself to think, by mental picture only, whether the pulling down of a certain tobacconist's shop (i. e. its *subtraction* from the row of houses in which it stands) would afford a good opening for a needed thoroughfare. Now, on first perceiving the image, it was associated with a mental perception of the *smell* of the shop. I inhibited that mental smell because it had nothing to do with what I wanted to think out. So words often arise in my own mind merely through association with what I am thinking about; they are *not* the things that my mind is dealing with; they are superfluous and they are embarrassments, so I inhibit them.

I have not yet inquired, but will do so, whether deaf-mutes who had never learnt words or any symbols for them, had ever been taught dominoes, or possibly even chess. I myself cannot conceive that the names—king, queen, etc.—are of any help in calculating a single move in advance. For the effect of many moves I use them mentally to record the steps gained, but for nothing else. I have reason to believe that not a few first-rate chess-players calculate by their mental eye only.

In speaking of modern mental literature, pray do not think me so conceited as to refer to my own writings only. I value modern above ancient literature on this subject, even if the modern writers are far smaller men than the older ones, because they have two engines of research which the others wanted:—

(1) Inductive inquiry, ethnological and other. The older authorities had no vivid conception of the different qualities of men's minds. They thought that a careful examination of their own minds sufficed for laying down laws that were generally applicable to humanity.

(2) They had no adequate notion of the importance of mental pathology. When by a blow, or by a disease, or, as they now say, by hypnotism, a whole province of mental faculties can be abolished, and the working of what remains can be carefully studied, it is now found that as good a clue to the anatomy of the mind may be obtained as men who study mangled limbs, or who systematically dissect, may obtain of the anatomy of the body.

I add nothing about the advantage to modern inquirers due to their possession of Darwinian facts and theories, because we do not rate them in the same way. Very truly yours,

Professor Max Müller. FRANCIS GALTON.

VIII. LETTER FROM PROF. MAX MÜLLER.

OXFORD, May 19, 1887.

MY DEAR MR. GALTON—If you think my letter worth publishing in *Nature*, I have no objection, though it contains no more than what anybody may read in my *Science of Thought.*

Nothing proves to my mind the dependence of thought on language so much as the difficulty we have in making others understand our thoughts by means of words. Take the instance you mention of a shop being pulled down in your street, and suggesting to you the desirability of opening a new street. There are races, or, at all events, there have been, who had no name or concept of shop. Still, if they saw your shop, they would call it a *house*, a *building*, a *cave*, a *hole*, or, as you suggest, a chamber of smells and horrors, but at all events a *thing*. Now, all these are names. Even *thing* is a name. Take away these names, and all definite thought goes; take away the name *thing*, and thought goes altogether. When I say word, I do not mean *flatus vocis*, I always mean word as inseparable from concept, thought-word or word-thought.

It is quite possible that you may *teach* deaf-and-dumb people dominoes; but deaf-and-dumb people, left to themselves, do not invent dominoes, and that makes a great difference. Even so simple a game as dominoes would be impossible without names and their underlying concepts. Dominoes are not mere blocks of wood; they signify something. This becomes much clearer in chess. You cannot move king, or queen, or knight as mere dolls. In chess, each one of these figures can be moved according to its name and concept only. Otherwise chess would be a chaotic scramble, not an intelligent game. If you once see what I mean by names, namely that by which a thing becomes *notum* or known, I expect you will say, "Of course we all admit that without a name we cannot really know anything."

I wonder you do not see that in all my writings I have been an evolutionist or Darwinian *pur sang*. What is language but a constant becoming? What is thought but an *Ewiges Werden?*

Everything in language begins by a personal habit, and then becomes inherited; but what we students of language try to discover is the first beginning of each personal habit, the origin of every thought, and the origin of every word. For that purpose ethnological researches are of the highest importance to us, and you will find that Kant, the cleverest dissector of abstract thought, was at the same time the most careful student of ethnology, the most accurate observer of concrete thought in its endless variety. With all my admiration for modern writers, I am in this sense also a Darwinian that I prefer the rudimentary stages of philosophic thought to its later developments, not to say its decadence. I have learnt more from Plato than from Comte. But I have ordered Binet all the same, and when I have read him I shall tell you what I think of him.

Yours very truly,

F. MAX MÜLLER.

IX. LETTER FROM MR. GEORGE J. ROMANES, F.R.S.

June 4, 1887.

There appears to be some ambiguity about this matter as discussed in the correspondence which has recently taken place in your columns. In the first instance Mr. Galton understood Professor Max Müller to have argued that in no individual human mind can any process of thought be ever conducted without the mental rehearsal of words, or the *verbum mentale* of the Schoolmen. Now, although this is the view which certainly appears to pervade the Professor's work on *The Science of Thought*, there is one passage in that work, and several passages in his subsequent correspondence with Mr. Galton, which express quite a different view—namely, that when a definite structure of conceptual ideation has been built up by the aid of words, it may afterward persist independently of such aid; the scaffolding was required for the original construction of the edifice, but not for its subsequent stability. That these two views are widely different may be shown by taking any one of the illustrations from the *Nature* correspondence. In answer to Mr. Galton, Professor Max Müller says: "It is quite possible that you may *teach* deaf-and-dumb people dominoes; but deaf-and-dumb people, left to themselves, do not *invent* dominoes, and that makes a great difference. Even so simple a game as dominoes would be impossible without names and their underlying concepts." Now, assuredly it does "make a great difference" whether we are supporting the view that dominoes could not be *played* without names underlying concepts, or the view that without such means dominoes could not have been *invented*. That there cannot be concepts without names is a well-recognized doctrine of psychology, and that dominoes could not have been invented in the absence of certain simple concepts relating to number no one could well dispute. But when the game has been invented, there is no need to fall back upon names and concepts as a preliminary to each move, or for the player to predicate to himself before each move that the number he lays down corresponds with the number to which he joins it. The late Dr. Carpenter assured me that he had personally investigated the case of a performing dog which was exhibited many years ago as a domino-player, and had fully satisfied himself that the animal's skill in this respect was genuine; i. e. not dependent on any code of signals from the showman. This, therefore, is a better case than that of the deaf-mute, in order to show that dominoes can be played by means of sensuous association alone. But my point now is that two distinct questions have been raised in your columns, and that the ambiguity to which I have referred appears to have arisen from a failure to distinguish between them. Every living psychologist will doubtless agree with Professor Max Müller where he appears to say nothing more than that if there had never been any names there could never have been any concepts; but this is a widely different thing from saying what he elsewhere appears to say;—i. e. that without the mental rehearsal of words there cannot be performed in any case a process of distinctively human thought. The first of these two widely different questions may be dismissed as one concerning which no difference of opinion is likely to arise. Touching the second, if the Professor does not mean what I have said he appears in some places to say, it is a pity that he should attempt to defend such a position as that chess, for instance, cannot be played unless the player "deals all the time with thought-words and word-thoughts." For the original learning of the game it was necessary that the powers of the various pieces should have been explained to him by means of words; but when this knowledge was thus gained it was no longer needful that before making any particular move he should mentally state the powers of all the pieces concerned, or predicate to himself the various possibilities which the move might involve. All these things he does by his specially-formed associations alone, just as does a draught-player, who is concerned with a much simpler order of relations; in neither case is any demand made upon the *verbum mentale.*

Again, if the Professor does not mean to uphold the view that in no case can there be distinctively human thought without the *immediate and direct* assistance of words, it is a mistake in him to represent "the dependence of thought on language" as absolute.* The full powers of conceptual ideation which belong to any individual man may or may not all have been due to words as used by his ancestors, his contemporaries and himself. But, however this may be, that these powers, when once attained, may afterward continue operative without the use of words is not a matter of mere opinion

*E. g.—"I hope I have thus answered everything that has been or that can possibly be adduced against what I call the fundamental tenet that the science of language, and what ought to become the fundamental tenet of the science of thought, namely, that language and thought, though distinguishable, are inseparable, that no one truly thinks who does not speak, and that no one truly speaks who does not think."—*Science of Thought*, pp. 63, 64.

based on one's own personal introspection, which no opponent can verify; it is a matter of objectively demonstrable fact, which no opponent can gainsay. For when a man is suddenly afflicted with aphasia he does not forthwith become as the thoughtless brute; he has lost all trace of words, but his reason may remain unimpaired.

GEORGE J. ROMANES.

X. LETTER FROM MR. J. J. MURPHY.

BELFAST, June 19, 1887.

I have postponed offering you any remarks on Professor Max Müller's *Science of Thought* until I had read the book through.

I think Prof. Max Müller is on the whole right, that language is necessary to thought, and is related to thought very much as organization to life. The question discussed by some of your correspondents, whether it is possible in particular cases to think without language, appears to me of little importance. I can believe that it is possible to think without words when the subjects of thought are visible things and their combinations, as in inventing machinery; but the intellectual power that invents machinery has been matured by the use of language.

But Prof. Max Müller has not answered, nor has he asked, the question, on what property or power of thought the production of language depends. He has shown most clearly the important truth that all names are abstract—that to invent a name which denotes an indefinite number of objects is a result of abstraction. But on what does the power of abstraction depend? I believe it depends on the power of directing thought at will. Prof. Max Müller lays stress on the distinction between percepts and concepts, though he thinks they are inseparable. I am inclined to differ from him, and to think that animals perceive as vividly as we do, but have only a rudimentary power of conception and thought. I think the power of directing thought at will is the distinctively human power, on which the power of forming concepts and language depends.

JOSEPH JOHN MURPHY.

XI. LETTER FROM MR. ARTHUR EBBELS.

CHAPHAN, June 6, 1887.

After reading the correspondence published in *Nature* (Vol. XXXVI. pp. 28, 52 and 100) on this subject, it has occurred to me that the difficulties anthropologists find in Professor Max Müller's theory are connected chiefly with his peculiar definitions.

In his letters to Mr. Galton, Prof. MaxMüller narrows the domain of his theory to a considerable extent. By defining thought as the faculty of "addition and subtraction," and by taking language as composed of "word-thoughts" or "thought-words," Prof. MaxMüller excludes from his theory all those processes which are preliminary to the formation of concepts. Thus narrowed, I do not see that his doctrine in any way touches the wider question, whether reasoning, as generally understood, is independent of language. If we keep to the terms of this theory, thoughts and words are undoubtedly inseparable. But this does not in the least imply that *all thought* is impossible without words.

When we enlarge the scope of our terms it is at once evident that thoughts and words are not inseparable. It is all very well to join together "thought-word" and "word-thought." Yet the thought is something quite distinct from the *mere sound* which stands as a word for it. A concept is formed from sensations. Our thoughts are occupied with what we see, and feel, and hear, and this primarily. Thus it is that, in the wider sense of thinking, we can *think in pictures.* This is the mental experience which Professor Tyndall so highly prizes. He likes to picture an imaginary process, not in words, not even by keeping words in the background, but in a mental presentation of the things themselves as they would affect his senses. Surely, then, if the mind can attend to its own reproduction of former sensations, and even form new arrangements of sensations for itself quite irrespective of word-signs, as Mr. Galton and most other thinkers have experienced, it is evident that thought and language are not inseparable.

All this is, of course, somewhat apart from Prof. Max Müller's restricted theory. But the question follows, how from these wider thoughts do we become possessed of the faculty of abstraction? Does not the one shade imperceptibly into the other? Prof. Max Müller answers no, and here I think he is at fault. It is at this point that anthropologists part company with him. If he be right, how do people learn? According to his theory new thoughts when they arise start into being under some general concept. I do not deny that they are placed under some general concept, but it seems to me that something entirely independent of the general concept has, for convenience, been placed under it, and this something must be *called a thought.* No doubt the thought is at first vague and indefinite, and only when it becomes definite does it require a name. But here one can plainly trace the genesis of a thought, and the adaptation of a word as a symbol for it. The new concept and its sign do not arise simultaneously. There are two distinct growths, not one only, as Prof. Max Müller's theory presupposes. The connection may be subtle and close, but the two elements can be easily separated. It avails nothing to say that until the thought is placed under a concept it is not a thought. This is a mere question of definition, not of actual fact.

I would point out one other consideration. If Prof. MaxMüller's theory were true for all kinds of thinking, development would be impossible. If man could not think without language, and could not have language without thinking, he would never have had either, except by a miracle. And scientific men will not accept the alternative. We can conceive shadowy thoughts gradually shaping to themselves a language for expression, and we can understand how each would improve the other, until by constant interaction a higher process of thought was introduced. But we cannot conceive the sudden appearance of the faculty of abstraction together with its ready-made signs or words.

I have often wished that Prof. MaxMüller would state distinctly how his theory accounts for the very first beginnings of language. I have not been able to discover any explanation of this point in his "Lectures on the Science of Language." ARTHUR EBBELS.

XII. LETTER FROM MRS. A. GRENFELL.

As poets have extraordinary inklings and *aperçus* on the most abstruse scientific questions, Wordsworth's opinion on this matter (quoted by De Quincey) is worth considering: Language is not the "*dress*" of thought, it is the "*incarnation.*" This is Shelley's *aperçu* of Darwinism. Man exists "but in the future and the past; being, not what he is, but what he has been and shall be." How to "distil working ideas from the obscurest poems"—to use Lord Acton's words—is one of the secrets of genius. A. GRENFELL.

XIII. LETTER FROM MR. ARTHUR NICOLS.

WATFORD, June 3, 1887.

The interesting discussion between Mr. Francis Galton and Prof. Max Müller on this subject will doubtless raise many questions in the minds of those who have paid some attention to the habits of animals. I have been asking myself whether, if Prof. Max Müller is right in his conclusion—"Of course we all admit that without a name we cannot really know anything" (an *utterable* name, I presume), and "one fact remains, animals have no language"—animals must not, therefore, be held by him incapable of knowing anything. This would bring us to the question whether animals *know* in the same manner as men, or in some other manner which men do not understand. Now, I think—at least it is as strong a conviction as I am capable of entertaining—that animals not only know, but deal with the materials of knowledge—facts—in a manner quite indistinguishable from the manner in which I mentally handle them myself. Thus, I place an animal in circumstances which are quite unfamiliar to it, and from which it is urgently pressed to escape. There are two, or perhaps three, courses open to it; one being, to my mind, patently the most advantageous. It tries all of them, and selects that which I should have chosen myself, though it is *much longer* in coming to its conclusion. Here the animal has the same facts as the man to deal with, and, after consideration and examination, its judgment precisely corresponds with the man's. I cannot, then, find it possible to deny that the mental operations are identical in *kind;* but that they are not so in *degree* can be demonstrated by my importing into the situation an element foreign to the experience of the animal, when its failure is certain. It makes no difference whether the animal is under stress, or acting voluntarily. It may frequently be found to choose the method which most recommends itself to the man's judgment. Every student of animals is familiar with numbers of such cases. Indeed they are constantly being recorded in the columns of *Nature*, and abound in all accepted works on animal intelligence. I am quite prepared to admit that where there are two or more courses open to it the animal will occasionally select that which presents the greatest difficulties and labor most assiduously to overcome them, sometimes trying the remaining courses and returning to that which it first chose. Darwin gives a good example of the honey-bee (*Origin of Species*, p. 225, edition 1872). But no one will be surprised at imperfect judgment or vacillation of will in an animal, when such are common among men.

Prof. Max Müller lays down the very distinct proposition that "animals have no language." I suppose *utterable* language is meant. Is this so? That their sign-language is both extensive and exact (and even understood to some extent as between widely different species) most naturalists, I apprehend, will entertain no doubt. But has any species an utterable language? What is to be the test of this? First there is the whole gamut of vocal expressions—which even we understand—conveying the ideas of *pain*, *pleasure*, *anger*, *warning*. What sportsman who has stalked extremely shy animals does not know the moment a bird or animal utters a certain note that he is discovered? If Prof. Max Müller will not admit this to be *language*, I for one, must ask him what it is. It conveys to others a distinct idea, in general if not in special terms, and seems to me quite equivalent to "Oh dear!" "This is nice" (expressed, I believe, in some African language by the reduplicated form *ñum-ñum*, the letter *n* having the same value as in the Spanish *mañana*), "Leave off," "Look out," "Come here," etc. Those who have heard animals calling to one another, particularly at night, and have carefully noted the modulations of their voices (why should there be modulations unless they have a definite value), will find it very hard to accept Prof. Max Müller's conclusion that "animals have no language." Every female mammal endowed with any kind of voice has the power of saying "Come here, my child," and it is an interesting fact beyond question that the knowledge of this call is feebly or not at all inherited, but must be impressed upon the young individual by experience. Further, the young brought up by an alien foster-mother pay no attention to the "Come here, my child," of the alien species. The clucking of the hen meets with no response from the ducklings she has reared, even when she paces frantically by the side of the pond imploring them not to commit suicide. But let us creep up under the banks of a sedgy pool at about this time of year. There swims a wild duck surrounded by her brood, dashing here and there at the rising *Phryganidæ*. Now let the frightful face of man peer through the sedges. A sharp "quack" from the duck, and her brood dive like stones, or plunge into the reeds. She, at least, knows what to say to them.

The already inordinate length of this letter precludes me from offering any instances of the communication of *specific* intelligence by means of the vocal organs of animals. I think it probable that we far underrate the vocabulary of animals from deficient attention—and, I speak for myself, stupidity. Possibly Prof. Max Müller has not yet examined "Sally," the black chimpanzee. If not, he would surely be much interested. She is by no means garrulous, but in spite of her poor vocal capacity, if he should still consider that she "cannot really know anything" on that account, I must have completely misinterpreted his letter to Mr. Galton.

ARTHUR NICOLS.

XIV. LETTER FROM PROF. MAX MÜLLER.

THE MOLT, SALCOMBE, July 4, 1887.

As I found that you had already admitted no less than thirteen letters on my recent work, *Science of Thought*, I hesitated for some time whether I ought to ask you to admit another communication on a subject which can be of interest to a very limited number of the readers of *Nature* only. I have, indeed, from the very beginning of my philological labors, claimed for the science of language a place among the physical sciences, and, in one sense, I do the same for the science of thought. Nature that does not include human nature in all its various manifestations would seem to me like St. Peter's without its cupola. But this plea of mine has not as yet been generally admitted. The visible material frame of man, his sense-organs and their functions, his nerves and his brain, all this has been recognized as the rightful domain of physical science. But beyond this physical science was not to go. There was the old line of separation, a line drawn by mediæval students between man, on one side, and his works, on the other; between the sense-organs and their perceptions; between the brain and its outcome, or, as it has sometimes been called, its secretion—namely, thought. To attempt to obliterate that line between physical science, on one side, and moral science, as it used to be called, on the other, was represented as mere confusion of thought. Still, here as elsewhere, a perception of higher unity does not necessarily imply an ignoring of useful distinctions. To me it has always seemed that man's nature can never be fully understood except as one and indivisible. His highest and most abstract thoughts appear to me inseparable from the lowest material impacts made upon his bodily frame. And "if nothing was ever in the intellect except what was first in the senses," barring, of course, the intellect itself, it follows that we shall never understand the working of the intellect, unless we first try to understand the senses, their organs, their functions, and in the end their products. For practical purposes, no doubt, we may, nay we ought, to separate the two. Thus, in my own special subject, it is well to separate the treatment of phonetics and acoustics from higher linguistic researches. We may call phonetics and acoustics the ground floor, linguistics the first story. But as every building is one—the ground floor purposeless without the first story, the first story a mere castle in the air without the ground floor—the science of man also is one, and would according to my opinion, be imperfect unless it included psychology in the widest meaning of that term, as well as physiology; unless it claimed the science of language and of thought, no less than the science of the voice, the ear, the nerves, and the brain, as its obedient vassals. It was, therefore, a real satisfaction to me that it should have been *Nature* where the questions raised in my *Science of Thought* excited the first interest, provoking strong opposition, and eliciting distinct approval, and I venture to crave your permission on that ground, if on no other, for replying once more to the various arguments which some of your most eminent contributors have brought forward against the fundamental tenet of my work, the inseparableness of language and reason.

Many of my critics write as if they had never heard before of the identity of language and reason. They call such a theory a paradox, unconscious, it would seem, of the fact that to the great majority of mankind all philosophy is a paradox, and unaware likewise, that the same opinion has been held by some of the greatest philosophers of antiquity, of the middle ages, and of modern times. I have not invented that paradox. All I have done or attempted to do is that, while other philosophers have derived their arguments in support of it from mere theory, I have taken mine from facts, namely the facts supplied by the science of language.

Some of my critics again seem to have sniffed something heterodox in this identity of language and reason, forgetting that philosophy was never meant to be either orthodox or heterodox in the theological sense of those words, and unaware likewise, as it would seem, that this opinion has been held and defended by some of the most orthodox and some of the most heterodox of modern writers. I shall mention two names only, Cardinal Newman and M. Taine. Cardinal Newman in his *Grammar of Assent* (p. 8), where he tries to define ratiocination or reasoning, begins by carefully separating from ratiocination, as I have done, all that is purely sensuous or emotional, the promptings of experience, common sense, genius, and all the rest, restricting "thought" to what can be or has been expressed in words. He then proceeds: "Let then our symbols be words; let all thought be arrested and embodied in words. Let language have a monopoly of thought; and thought go for only so much as it can show itself to be worth in language. Let every prompting of the intellect be ignored, every *momentum* of argument be disowned which is unprovided with an equivalent wording, as its ticket for sharing in the common search after truth. Let the authority of actions, common sense, experience, genius, go for nothing. Ratiocination thus restricted and put into grooves, is what I have called *Inference*, and the science which is its regulating principle, is *Logic*."

M. Taine pronounces quite as explicitly in favor of the theory that reasoning, if properly restricted and defined, takes place by means of words only, and cannot take place in any other way. In his work, *De l'Intelligence* (1870), after distinguishing between *proper* and *common* names, he shows that a common name is at the same time *general* and *abstract* (Vol. I. p. 25), and that these general and abstract names are really what we mean by general and abstract ideas. "Partout ce que nous appelons une idée générale née d'en semble, n'est qu'un nom; non pas le simple son qui vibre dans l'air et ébranle notre oreille, ou l'assemblage de lettres qui noircisseut le papier et frappent nos yeux, non pas même ces lettres aperçues mentalement, ou ce son mentalement prononcé, mais ce son ou ces lettres doué, lorsque nous les apercevons ou imaginons, d'une propriété double, la propriété d'éveiller en nous les images des individus qui appartiennent à une certaine classe de ces individus seulement, et la propriété de renaître toutes les fois qu'un individu de cette même classe et seulement quand un individu de cette même classe se présente à notre mémoire ou à notre expérience."

"Ce ne sout pas les objets épais ni les objets idéaux que nous pensons,—mais les caractères abstraits qui sout leurs générateurs; ce ne sout pas les caractères abstraits que nous pensons, mais les noms communs qui leur correspondent!"

I may divide the letters published hitherto in *Nature* into three classes, unanswerable, answered and to be answered.

I class as unanswerable such letters as that of the Duke of Argyll. His Grace simply expresses his opinion, without assigning any reasons. I do not deny that to myself personally, and to many of your readers, it is of great importance to know what position a man of the Duke's wide experience and independence of thought takes with regard to the fundamental principle of all philosophy, the identity of language and thought, or even on a merely subsidiary question, such as the genealogical descent of man from any known or unknown kind of animal. But I must wait till the Duke controverts either the linguistic facts, or the philosophical lessons which I have read in them, before I can meet fact by fact, and argument by argument. I only note, as a very significant admission, one sentence of his letter, in which the Duke says: "Language seems to me to be necessary to *the progress of thought*, but not at all necessary to the mere act of thinking." This sentence may possibly concede all that I have been contending for, as we shall see by and by.

I class as letters that have been answered the very instructive communications from Mr. F. Galton, to which I replied in *Nature* of June 2 (p. 101), as well as several notes contributed by correspondents who evidently had read my book either very rapidly, or not at all.

Thus, Hyde Clarke tells us that the mutes at Constantinople, and the deaf-mutes in general, communicate by signs, and not by words—the very fact on which I had laid great stress in several parts of my book. In the sign-language of the American Indians, in the hieroglyphic inscriptions of Egypt, and in Chinese and other languages which were originally written ideographically, we have irrefragable evidence that other signs, besides vocal signs or vocables, can be used for embodying thought. This, as I tried to show, confirms, and does not invalidate, my theory that we cannot think without words, if only it is remembered that words are the most usual and the most perfect, but by no means the only possible signs.

Another correspondent, "S. F. M. Q.", asks how I account for the early processes of thought in a deaf-mute. If he had looked at page 63 of my book, he would have found my answer. Following Professor Huxley, I hold that deaf-mutes would be capable of few higher intellectual manifestations than an orang or chimpanzee, if they were confined to the society of dumb associates.

But, though holding this opinion, I do not venture to say that deaf-mutes, if left to themselves, may not act rationally, as little as I should take upon myself to assert that animals may not act rationally. I prefer indeed, as I have often said, to remain a perfect agnostic with regard to the inner life of animals, and, for that, of deaf-mutes also. But I should not contradict anybody who imagines that he has discovered traces of the highest intellectual and moral activity in deaf-mutes or animals. I read with the deepest interest the letter which Mr. Arthur Nicols addressed to you. I accept all he says about the sagacity of animals, and if I differ from him at all, I do so because I have even greater faith in animals than he has. I do not think, for instance, that animals, as he says, are much longer in arriving at a conclusion than we are. Their conclusions, so far as I have been able to watch them, seem to me far more rapid than our own, and almost instantaneous. Nor should I quarrel with Mr. Nicols if he likes to call the vocal expressions of pain, pleasure, anger, or warning, uttered by animals, language. It is a perfectly legitimate metaphor to call every kind of communication language.

We may speak of the language of the eyes, and even of the eloquence of silence. But Mr. Nicols would probably be equally ready to admit that there is a difference between shouting "Oh!" and saying "I am surprised." An animal may say "Oh!" but it cannot say "I am surprised;" and it seems to me necessary, for the purpose of accurate reasoning, to be able to distinguish in our terminology between these two kinds of communication. On this point, too, I have so fully dwelt in my book that I ought not to encumber your pages by mere extracts.

I now come to the letters of Mr. Ebbels and Mr. Mellard Reade. They both seem to imagine that, because I deny the possibility of conceptual thought without language, I deny the possibility of every kind of thought without words. This objection, too, they will find so fully answered in my book, that I need not add anything here. I warned my readers again and again against the promiscuous use of the word "thought." I pointed out (p. 29) how, according to Descartes, any kind of inward activity, whether sensation, pain, pleasure, dreaming, or willing, may be called thought; but I stated on the very first page that, like Hobbes, I use thinking in the restricted sense of adding and subtracting. We do many things, perhaps our best things, without addition or subtraction. We have, as I pointed out on page 20, sensations and percepts, as well as concepts and names. For ordinary purposes we should be perfectly correct in saying that we can "think in pictures." This, however, is more accurately called imagination, because we are then dealing with images, presentations (*Vorstellungen*), or, as I prefer to call them, percepts and not yet with concepts and names. Whether in man and particularly in the present stage of his intellectual life, imagination is possible without a slight admixture of conceptual thought and language, is a moot point; that it is possible in animals, more particularly in Sally, the black chimpanzee at the Zoölogical Gardens, I should be reluctant either to deny or to affirm. All I stand up for is that, if we use such words as thought, we ought to define them. Definition is the only panacea for all our philosophical misery, and I am utterly unable to enter into Mr. Ebbels's state of mind when he says: "This is a mere question of definition, not of actual fact."

When Mr. Ebbels adds that we cannot conceive the sudden appearance of the faculty of abstraction together with its ready-made signs or words, except by a miracle, he betrays at once that he has not read my last book, the very object of which is to show that we require no miracle at all, but that all which seemed miraculous in language is perfectly natural and intelligible. And if he adds that he has not been able to discover in my earlier works any account of the first beginnings of language, he has evidently overlooked the fact that in my lectures on the science of language I distinctly declined to commit myself to any theory on the origin of language, while the whole of my last book is devoted to the solution of that problem. My solution may be right or wrong, but it certainly does not appeal to any miraculous interference for the explanation of language and thought.

There now remain two letters only that have really to be answered, because they touch on some very important points, points which it is manifest I ought to have placed in a clearer light in my book. One is by Mr. Murphy, the other by Mr. Romanes. Both have evidently read my book and read it carefully; and if they have not quite clearly seen the drift of my argument, I am afraid the fault is mine and not theirs. I am quite aware that my *Science of Thought* is not an easy book to read and to understand. I warned my readers in the preface that they must not expect a popular book, nor a work systematically built up and complete in all its parts. My book was written, as I said, for myself and for a few friends who knew beforehand the points which I wished to establish, and who would not expect me, for the mere sake of completeness, to repeat what was familiar to them and could easily be found elsewhere. I felt certain that I should be understood by them, if I only indicated what I meant; nor did it ever enter into my mind to attempt to teach them, or to convince them against their will. I wrote as if in harmony with my readers, and moving on with them on a road which we had long recognized as the only safe one, and which I hoped that others also would follow, if they could once be made to see whence it started and whither it tended.

Mr. Murphy is one of those who agree with me that language is necessary to thought, and that, though it may be possible to think without words when the subjects of thought are visible things and their combinations, as in inventing machinery, the intellectual power that invents machinery has been matured by the use of language. Here Mr. Murphy comes very near to the remark made by the Duke of Argyll, that language seems necessary to the *progress of thought*, but not at all necessary to the mere act of thinking, whatever that may mean. But Mr. Murphy, while accepting my two positions—that thought is impossible without words, and that all words were in their origin abstract—blames me for not having explained more fully on what the power of abstraction really depends. So much has lately been written on abstraction, that I did not think it necessary to do more than indicate to which side I inclined. I quoted the opinions of Aristotle, Bacon, Locke, Berkeley and Mill, and as for myself I stated in one short sentence that I should ascribe the power of abstraction, not so much to an effort of our will, or to our intellectual strength, but rather to our intellectual weakness. In forming abstractions our weakness seems to me our strength. Even in our first sensations it is impossible for us to take in the whole of every impression, and in our first perceptions we cannot but drop a great deal of what is contained in our sensations. In this sense we learn to abstract, whether we like it or not; and though afterwards abstraction may proceed from an effort of the will, I still hold, as I said on page 4, that though *attention* can be said to be at the root of all our knowledge, the power of abstraction may in the beginning not be very far removed from the weakness of distraction. If I had wished to write a practical text-book of the science of thought, I ought no doubt to have given more prominence to this view of the origin of abstraction, but as often in my book, so here too, I thought *sapienti sat.*

I now come to Mr. Romanes, to whom I feel truly grateful for the intrepid spirit with which he has waded through my book. One has no right in these days to expect many such readers, but one feels all the more grateful if one does find them. Mr. Romanes was at home in the whole subject, and with him what I endeavored to prove by linguistic evidence—namely, that concepts are altogether impossible without names—formed part of the very A B C of his psychological creed. He is indeed almost too sanguine when he says that concerning this truth no difference of opinion is likely to arise. The columns of *Nature* and the opinions quoted in my book tell a different tale. But for all that I am as strongly convinced as he can be that no one who has once understood the true nature of words and concepts can possibly hold a different opinion from that which he holds as well as I.

It seems, therefore, all the more strange to me that Mr. Romanes should have suspected me of holding the opinion that we cannot think without pronouncing or silently rehearsing our thought-words. It is difficult to guard against misapprehensions which one can hardly realize. Without appealing, as he does, to sudden aphasia, how could I hold pronunciation necessary for thought when I am perfectly silent while I an writing and while I am reading? How could

I believe in the necessity of a silent rehearsing of words when one such word as "therefore" may imply hundreds of words or pages, the rehearsing of which would require hours and days? Surely, as our memory enables us to see without eyes and to hear without ears, the same persistence of force allows us to speak without uttering words. Only, as we cannot remember or imagine without having first seen or heard something to remember, neither can we inwardly speak without having first named something that we can remember. There is an algebra of language far more wonderful than the algebra of mathematics. Mr. Romanes calls that algebra "ideation," a dangerous word, unless we first define its meaning and lay bare its substance. I call the same process addition and subtraction of half-vanished words, or, to use Hegel's terminology, *aufgehobene Worte;* and I still hold, as I said in my book, that it would be difficult to invent a better expression for thinking than that of the lowest barbarians, "speaking in the stomach." Thinking is nothing but speaking *minus* words. We do not begin with thinking or *ideation*, and then proceed to speaking, but we begin with naming, and then by a constant process of addition and subtraction, of widening and abbreviating, we arrive at what I call thought. Everybody admits that we cannot count—that is to say, add and subtract—unless we have first framed our numerals. Why should people hesitate to admit that we cannot possibly think, unless we have first formed our words? Did the Duke of Argyll mean this when he said that language seemed to him necessary for *the progress of thought*, but not at all for the mere act of thinking? How words are framed, the science of language has taught us; how they are reduced to mere shadows, to signs of signs, apparently to mere nothings, the science of thought will have to explain far more fully than I have been able to do. Mr. Romanes remarks that it is a pity that I should attempt to defend such a position as that chess cannot be played unless the player "deals all the time with thought-words and word-thoughts." I pity myself indeed that my language should be liable to such misapprehension. I thought that to move a "castle" according to the character and the rules originally assigned to it was to deal with a word-thought or thought-word. What is "castle" in chess, if not a word-thought or thought-word? I did not use the verb "to deal" in the sense of pronouncing, or rehearsing, or defining, but of handling or moving according to understood rules. That this dealing might become a mere habit I pointed out myself, and tried to illustrate by the even more wonderful playing of music. But however automatic and almost unconscious such habits may become, we have only to make a wrong move with the "castle" and at once our antagonist will appeal to the original meaning of that thought-word and remind us that we can move it in one direction only, but not in another. In the same manner, when Mr. Romanes takes me to task because I said that "no one truly thinks who does not speak, and that no one truly speaks who does not think," he had only to lay the accent on *truly*, and he would have understood what I meant—namely, that in the true sense of these words, as defined by myself, no one thinks who does not directly or indirectly speak, and that no one can be said to speak who does not at the same time think. We cannot be too charitable in the interpretation of language, and I often feel that I must claim that charity more than most writers in English. Still, I am always glad if such opponents as Mr. Romanes or Mr. F. Galton give me an opportunity of explaining more fully what I mean. We shall thus, I believe, arrive at the conviction that men who honestly care for truth, and for the progress of truth, must in the end arrive at the same conclusions, though they may express them each in his own dialect. That is the true meaning of the old dialectic process, to reason out things by words more and more adequate to their purpose. In that sense it is true also that no truth is entirely new, and that all we can aim at in philosophy is to find new and better expressions for old truths. The poet, as Mrs. A. Grenfell has pointed out in her letter to *Nature* (June 23, p. 173), often perceives and imagines what others have not yet conceived or named. In that sense I gladly call myself the interpreter of Wordsworth's prophecy, that "the word is not the dress of thought, but its very incarnation."

F. MAX MÜLLER.

CATALOGUE OF PUBLICATIONS

OF THE

OPEN COURT PUBLISHING CO.

COPE, E. D.

THE PRIMARY FACTORS OF ORGANIC EVOLUTION.
121 cuts. Pp. xvi, 547. Cloth, $2.00 net (10s.).

MÜLLER, F. MAX.

THREE INTRODUCTORY LECTURES ON THE SCIENCE OF THOUGHT.
128 pages. Cloth, 75c (3s. 6d.).

THREE LECTURES ON THE SCIENCE OF LANGUAGE.
112 pages. 2nd Edition. Cloth, 75c (3s. 6d.).

ROMANES, GEORGE JOHN.

DARWIN AND AFTER DARWIN.
An Exposition of the Darwinian Theory and a Discussion of Post-Darwinian Questions. Three Vols., $4.00 net. Singly, as follows:
1. THE DARWINIAN THEORY. 460 pages. 125 illustrations. Cloth, $2 00.
2. POST-DARWINIAN QUESTIONS. Heredity and Utility. Pp. 338. $1.50.
3. POST-DARWINIAN QUESTIONS. Isolation and Physiological Selection. Pp. 181. $1.00.

AN EXAMINATION OF WEISMANNISM.
236 pages. Cloth, $1 00 net.

THOUGHTS ON RELIGION.
Edited by Charles Gore, M. A., Canon of Westminster. Third Edition, Pages, 184. Cloth, gilt top, $1.25 net.

MACH, ERNST.

THE SCIENCE OF MECHANICS.
A CRITICAL AND HISTORICAL EXPOSITION OF ITS PRINCIPLES. Translated by T. J. McCORMACK. 250 cuts. 534 pages. ½ m., gilt top. $2.50 (12s.6d.).

POPULAR SCIENTIFIC LECTURES.
Third Edition. 415 pages. 59 cuts. Cloth, gilt top. Net, $1.50 (7s. 6d.)

THE ANALYSIS OF THE SENSATIONS.
Pp. 208. 37 cuts. Cloth, $1.25 net (6s. 6d.).

LAGRANGE, J. L.

LECTURES ON ELEMENTARY MATHEMATICS.
With portrait of the author. Pp. 172. Price, $1 00 net (5s.).

DE MORGAN, AUGUSTUS.

ON THE STUDY AND DIFFICULTIES OF MATHEMATICS.
New Reprint edition with notes. Pp. viii+288. Cloth, $1.25 net (5s.)

SCHUBERT, HERMANN.

MATHEMATICAL ESSAYS AND RECREATIONS.
Pp. 149. Cuts, 37. Cloth, 75c net (3s. 6d.).

HUC AND GABET, MM.

TRAVELS IN TARTARY, THIBET AND CHINA.
(1844-1846.) Translated from the French by W. Hazlitt. Illustrated with 100 engravings on wood. 2 vols. Pp. 28 + 660. Cl., $2.00 (10s.)

CORNILL, CARL HEINRICH.

THE PROPHETS OF ISRAEL.
Popular Sketches from Old Testament History. Pp., 200 Cloth, $1.00 net (5s.).

HISTORY OF THE PEOPLE OF ISRAEL.
Pp. vi + 325. Cloth, $1.50 (7s. 6d.).

POWELL, J. W.

TRUTH AND ERROR; or, the Science of Intellection.
Pp. 423. Cloth, $1.75 (7s. 6d.).

WAGNER, RICHARD.

A PILGRIMAGE TO BEETHOVEN.
A Story. With portrait of Beethoven. Pp. 40. Boards, 50c net (2s. 6d.)

HUTCHINSON, WOODS.

THE GOSPEL ACCORDING TO DARWIN.
Pp. xii + 241. Price, $1.50 (6s.).

FREYTAG, GUSTAV.

THE LOST MANUSCRIPT. A Novel.
2 vols. 953 pages. Extra cloth, $4.00 (21s). One vol., cl., $1.00 (5s.).

MARTIN LUTHER.
Illustrated. Pp. 130. Cloth, $1.00 net (5s.).

TRUMBULL, M. M.

THE FREE TRADE STRUGGLE IN ENGLAND.
Second Edition. 296 pages. Cloth, 75c (3s. 6d.).

WHEELBARROW: ARTICLES AND DISCUSSIONS ON THE LABOR QUESTION
With portrait of the author. 303 pages. Cloth, $1.00 (5s.).

GOETHE AND SCHILLER'S XENIONS.

Translated by Paul Carus. Album form. Pp. 162. Cl., $1.00 (5s.).

OLDENBERG, H.

ANCIENT INDIA: ITS LANGUAGE AND RELIGIONS.
Pp. 100. Cloth, 50c net (2s. 6d.).

CARUS, PAUL.

THE ETHICAL PROBLEM.
Second edition, revised and greatly enlarged. 351 pages. Cloth, $1.25 (6s. 6d.).

FUNDAMENTAL PROBLEMS.
Second edition, enlarged and revised. 372 pp. Cl., $1.50 (7s. 6d.).

HOMILIES OF SCIENCE.
317 pages. Cloth, Gilt Top, $1.50 (7s. 6d.).

THE IDEA OF GOD.
Fourth edition. 32 pages. Paper, 15c (9d.).

THE SOUL OF MAN.
With 152 cuts and diagrams. 458 pages. Cloth, $3.00 (15s.).

TRUTH IN FICTION. TWELVE TALES WITH A MORAL.
White and gold binding, gilt edges. Pp. 111. $1.00 (5s.).

THE RELIGION OF SCIENCE.
Second, extra edition. Pp. 103. Price, 50c net (2s. 6d.).

PRIMER OF PHILOSOPHY.
240 pages. Second Edition. Cloth, $1.00 (5s.).

THE GOSPEL OF BUDDHA. According to Old Records.
Fifth Edition. Pp. 275. Cloth, $1.00 (5s.). In German, $1.25 (6s. 6d.)

BUDDHISM AND ITS CHRISTIAN CRITICS.
Pages, 311. Cloth, $1.25 (6s. 6d.).

KARMA. A STORY OF EARLY BUDDHISM.
Illustrated by Japanese artists. Crêpe paper, 75c (3s. 6d.).

NIRVANA: A STORY OF BUDDHIST PSYCHOLOGY.
Japanese edition, like *Karma*. $1.00 (4s. 6d.).

LAO-TZE'S TAO TEH-KING.
Chinese-English. With introduction, transliteration, Notes, etc. Pp 360. Cloth, $3.00 (15s.).

GARBE, RICHARD.

THE REDEMPTION OF THE BRAHMAN. A TALE OF HINDU LIFE.
Laid paper. Gilt top. 96 pages. Price, 75c (3s. 6d.).

THE PHILOSOPHY OF ANCIENT INDIA.
Pp. 89. Cloth, 50c net (2s. 6d.).

HUEPPE, FERDINAND.

THE PRINCIPLES OF BACTERIOLOGY.
28 Woodcuts. Pp. 467 + x. Price, $1.75 net (9s.).